TASTE OF ENLIGHTENMENT

Attaining the inner Divinity

Mahesh

Made with ♥ on the Notion Press Platform
www.notionpress.com

Special Mention :

The cover image and the images in the interior are assets from Freepik.com

Contents

Preface 7

1. On Reality 11

2. On 'The Experiencer' 20

3. Maturity and Enlightenment 27

4. Axle of the Wheel of Thoughts 31

5. The Mind and its control 37

6. The seer and the seen 45

7. On Consciousness 51

8. Fate 56

9. Renunciation 63

Preface

This book essentially deals with spiritualism and fundamental Truth of sentient beings.

It highlights, that in whatever condition one is, one always 'thinks,' not because 'thinking' is essential at all moments, but because 'thinking' has become an addiction.

It asserts that attaining the true knowledge, emancipates a human being from the clutches of illusion and flooding thoughts, paving way for peace to be.

The author has written this book out of his own experience of the divine truth.

The book primarily proposes "surrender" to the supreme reality, as a means to "Satsang" (association with the supreme Lord.)

Author,
Mahesh.

NOW,

IN THE NAME OF THAT HOLINESS;

IN THE NAME OF THAT ETERNAL DIVINE BEING;

IN THE NAME OF THAT MIGHTY TRUTH;

"Satsang" is being expounded…

Chapter 1

On Reality

Throughout the ages, human beings have believed that there is a higher force, which has created everything and leads everyone to their destiny. And there are others who disbelieve it. Even the one who believes in the higher force and the non-believers as well, are compatible in the conviction that they live "By Choice."

One is convinced that they think and act by their own choice and will. This conviction is so firm that one denounces the contrary exposition.

To realize whether we live "By Choice" or "By Chance," whether there exists a higher force or not, possessing a "Belief" will not suffice. A meticulous, sincere investigation is demanded for the stupendous Truth to surface.

The belief of free-will, that we act and think by our choice, leads to the creation of various philosophies, by various minds, at various times all of which have created various sects. Since the whole labyrinth of philosophies are grounded in the ideology of human "Action," it is imperative to explore this matter of "Action" vividly, completely and absolutely.

The term Action implies the movement; movement of body and mind.

To behold the movement of one's body and mind is to comprehend the truth of Action. The activities of one's body such as walking, sitting, lifting arms, turning the head, speaking and so on are considered to be the actions of one's choice and will. First of all, if one observes, the physical body is capable of acting due to the occurrence of breath, circulation of blood and of the proper functioning of inner organs. If one notices one's breath, one could realize that breathing happens automatically and that it is not one's "Doing." Similarly, the circulation of blood and the function of each and every inner organ of the body are not one's "Doing," but an automatic happening.

Without these automatic activities of breath and the organs of body, could one walk, sit, lift one's arm, and turn the head? Therefore, what one calls a "Choice" to walk or sit, is grounded in and supported by something higher than oneself, within oneself. The whole of one's body is apparently acting under the influence of something superior than oneself. That 'Superior,' which is breathing is the sole reason for even the superficial tiny finger movement of one's body.

The real doer:

When you were a small child, you did not have any identity as "I am." Your breath, hands, legs, eyes, head, everything moved and acted on their own accord.

You were not the "Doer" of any of your bodily movement. The same body that had automatically breathed, digested, excreted, sweated, slept and woke, starts growing. After a period of time, a personality or identity comes into existence as "I am." After having sensed the "I am" as a personality, you start identifying and associating that "I am" with the body, that was already automatically breathing, digesting, excreting, sweating, sleeping, waking, moving and acting. Consequently, you start identifying those automatic orderly actions of the body as 'Your' actions. If the head turns automatically, you think that 'you' have turned it. If your hand grabs something, you think that 'you' are grabbing it. If that body is afraid of something due to its protective nature, you think that 'you' are afraid and so on and so forth.

But in the actuality, the same higher force, that was breathing, lifting the arms, shaking the legs, crying, smiling when you were a child is still the "Doer" of all these things, now too. You have not succeeded that higher power at any point of time, nor has the higher power transformed its authority of the body to you.

But, why do you have the firm conviction that you are acting your body? That is because, before your hand grabs something, you have been given a thought of grabbing it. A spark of thought flashes in you, before the body acts. When you were a child, the same hand grabbed something without having a forethought about it. But now, the same hand grabs following a thought. Since you identify with the thought that flashes in you as "Your" thought, makes you feel that 'you' are acting the body.

What is the source of thoughts? Whence it is? Are thoughts really under one's control? Does one really think by one's choice and will, or does thoughts automatically occur in oneself? If one believes that one consciously and willfully thinks, then why couldn't one possess the power to control thoughts? Are we controlling thoughts or does thoughts control us? The conviction that one thinks by their choice, is mere an illusion.

If one observes very carefully in oneself, one could clearly see that a thought is prior to one's attention to it. It is after a thought arises automatically, one's attention falls on it. We are aware of a thought only after it has risen. Only after an infinitesimal of a second later to the occurrence of a thought, one becomes aware of it. Since the automatically arising "Thought" and our "Awareness" merges so swiftly, we assume that we are attentively thinking by our choice. The conviction that "I am thinking" arises due to this swift inward happening.

Consciousness that exists as "I am," resides amidst the automatic movements of the body and the automatic occurrence of thoughts.

As the physical body is governed and moved by the higher power, thoughts too crop up from the same higher power.

The "I am" is pure "Attention" or "Consciousness" only.

What is a "Vessel" exactly? Is vessel a form or an empty space within that form? If a vessel is filled with water, where does exactly the water get filled? Is it in the emptiness or in the form? It is in the emptiness of the vessel that the water is being filled.

Hence, a vessel is an emptiness in reality; the structure that surrounds the emptiness is a support for the water not to spill. According to the fencing structure of the emptiness, we name something as a pot, something as a cup, something as a bin, something as a nest, something as a house and so on; various names for that one emptiness. Emptiness is the source of everything. Similarly, one's real "I am" is an indistinguishable "Attention" fenced by the body and filled with thoughts.

What is one's "I am" as of now? For an instance, if we wipe away all the memories of a particular human being from his brain through an electric device or so, how will he behave then? Could he assert who is he after his memory is deleted? If we ask him 'who are you,' can he reply his identity? The same previous "I am" does not exist in him now. So, what is precisely one's "I am" as of now? One's "I am" is nothing but one's memories. If thoughts as memories are deleted, the "I am" is also deleted.

When you were a small child, you completely lived at the moment without thought or memory. Thoughts did not occupy you then. That's why you were able to be so attentive to every details around you. You lived without an "I am" as a personality in particular. By and by, the happenings are registered by the brain and that becomes memory. And when the memory as thought manifested, a past has happened. With the past, an "I am" as a personality or identity has arrived. The deletion of your past is the deletion of your personality "I am." Therefore, "I am" is nothing but "Thoughts" or "Past."

This "Thought" created "I am" is illusive and fictitious. It acts as a veil upon the real "I am" that is pure "Attention" or "Witness." On suspending this illusive "I am," which is of the past, one encounters one's real "I am" that exists always in the "Now." The fictitious "I am" has its roots in the past, whereas the real "I am" is rooted all the time in the "Now."

To suspend the illusive "I am" and to encounter the real "I am," one should watch oneself as one watches the other person. How would we usually watch the other person? Will we not look at their face expression and body's movement? In the exact manner one should watch one's own "expressions" in all the situations. While experiencing happiness, suffering, anger, fear, frustration, anxiety, laughter or joy, one should watch one's own face and body as to how it expresses automatically to the situation. One should attentively watch the expressions of one's own eyes, mouth, tongue and fingers in particular. It should be a sudden watch of your face and fingers of your hands (not in the mirror) and should continue that watching for a few minutes. Then the expressions become still; yet one should continue watching that stillness of one's face and body and be with that stillness. Association with that stillness is association with the supreme beyond.

If a person starts doing this, then she or he does a great thing, which is nameless. However, if one is to name this act, then it is called **SATSANG** (Association with the Supreme Truth).

From thereon "HE," the most Sacred, the most Holy, Possessor of eternal smile, who is eternally anew, Who is beyond Time, will take hold of you and walk in your walking; stand in your standing; sits magnificently in your sitting and do in your Doing. He will make you realize that HE is the Doer and not you. The action which comes out of you will be "through" you and not "from" you. Realization of this automatically leads to "Surrender" to that Absolute Being.

Chapter 2

On 'The Experiencer'

Experience is what we always long for – to be it joyful, pleasurable perpetually.

Since wanting of experience is the prime craving of a human being, it is of utmost importance to have an insight into "Who is experiencing," rather than the "Experience" itself. As long as one is in conscious state, one always experiences something, either by will or by involuntary happening. Experience isn't possible in the unconscious state like deep sleep and swoon. Hence, to behold the consciousness is to unravel the mystery of "the experiencer."

Be it happiness, sorrow or fear – who is experiencing it?

Who is experiencing a dream in your sleep? Dream occurs in sleep due to the forgetfulness of one's true identity. It is due to the oblivion of the self, dream emerges as an experience. If one wakes up suddenly from sleep, the experience of dream ceases instantaneously since one becomes conscious of one's true self. Therefore, "Experience" as such contrasts or is incompatible to "Self Consciousness."

While dream occurs in your sleep, you forget that you are sleeping. In that dream, you see an event is taking place. You may see a street, line of houses, people moving, and animals strolling over somewhere and so on. Within that scenario, you will see "YOU" also standing somewhere, wearing a particular coloured dress, standing in a particular pose and talking to your friends. Suppose a dog jumps over and chases you and your friends, you all will split and run.

The fear experienced by you at that instant is real; you are real, the dog is real, and the street, houses, people and their voices all are real. Now, who is really affected by the fear and who is experiencing the whole phenomena? Is it not to a dream personality? Are you really that dream person or the person who is asleep in bed is the real "You?"

The person who saw the dog and ran, resembling you is the real Experiencer; not the real "You," who is sleeping on the bed. When you wake up from bed, you start realizing that the dog, street, people and the fear are unreal and fictitious. The most essential thing to realize is, the "YOU" that existed in that dream, is equally a fictitious entity. That particular fictitious entity is the "Experiencer." In all of one's dreams, that fictitious "I" is the experiencer and not the real "I." Now, who is the 'experiencer' in the wakeful state? Suppose you experience fear in the wakeful state, do you really experience it? Or does the same fictitious dream "I" experience? The same dream "I" which was experiencing in the dream with a dream body still exists subtly and experiences in the wakeful state too. We term that event as **"THOUGHTS,"** in the wakeful state. When you experience fear in your wakeful state, you are thinking of an imaginary fearful scene, where you may bring in an imaginary person, an imaginary house, imaginary object of fear, an imaginary place and also you bring along an imaginary "YOU" in that scene, and that particular imaginary "YOU" starts experiencing the fear, as same as it occurred in the dream. The experience of happiness, sorrow and even the small details of day to day experience happens only thus. If one starts seeing the beauty of this, then the immaculate original Self with its magnificence, directs the course of one's life.

In the state of your suffering, do you really suffer or are you thinking that you are suffering?

While suffering, you project a thought. In that field of thought, you may see a street, a house or some place, where you see someone over there and at the same time you see "YOU" also present in that place and talking to that someone, as same as it occurred in the dream. In that situation, the fictitious "YOU" that is present, experiences the suffering with expressions in its fictitious face. The real face of yours do not do expressions, although ripples of vibration is concomitant. The "I" thought in awakening state and the dream "I" in slumber are the real sufferers. The real "YOU" is simply a witness in both of these states. If one directs one's attention upon oneself, one can distinctly realize these happenings. Mind is the experience and the 'experiencer' both; not consciousness. Consciousness is the real "I."

When you see a friend in your thought, two things are present in the realms of that thought; one is the imaginary friend and the other is the imaginary "YOU."

The **Friend** and **You** both are equally Imagination. Basically, we have the conviction that the friend is an imagination in our thought, but the "I" is real. Whereas in actuality if one discerns the Truth through pure observation, the "I" as an 'Experiencer' is equally an imagination. Realization of this, quells the imaginary "I."

The "Experience" is a thought and the "Experiencer" is also a thought.

The real "YOU" is a silent spectator.

Not letting the fictitious "I" in one's thought, at least for three minutes, either by way of control or by being aware, one is faced with the beauty of one's own pure, uncontaminated "I" that is garlanded with indestructible silence.

Chapter 3

Maturity and Enlightenment

If one remembers the sorrows of one's childhood days, as it were, the same sorrows do not trouble now, even if provided with the same problems. The problem that brought in sorrow on losing a doll, a want of toy, or a conflict with a friend and the like do not trouble one's mind anymore, when one becomes an adolescent.

With regard to relationship with the doll, a child names it, dresses it up, gives life to it, and considers the doll as its friend or sibling.

The child hugs it, protects it, possesses it and experiences happiness, joy, and sorrow in accordance with the degree of attachment. When the same child becomes an adolescent, the entire feeling for that doll is nullified. Likewise, the problems and sorrows of adolescent stage do not trouble a person when one becomes an adult.

Since an adult has transcended the problems and sorrows of his own childhood and adolescent stage, that does not mean in any way, that the adult has transcended by discovering a proper solution to the problems of his childhood and adolescence. The problems and sorrows have not ended up by discovering solutions to them, but rather they have simply ended by themselves, when one grows as an adult. It is the growth in maturity from childhood to adolescence, then from adolescence to adulthood that gives solution. On being in the same plane of existence, cessation of sorrow or fear becomes impossible, because the attitude of a particular stage is the outcome of the same level of maturity or conscious level.

A child projects a life upon a doll and prisons its experience by perceiving its own projection. Similarly, all the subsequent growth in maturity projects a life upon an outward object or entity, and prisons its experience by perceiving its own projection. In dream one encounters a nightmare and is afraid, because one's consciousness exists within the same field of that dream. Eradication of fear or sorrow is impossible while being on the same field of maturity. The fear or sorrow in a dream vanishes only on waking up from sleep.

Hence, the problems and sorrows can be uprooted only by shifting the consciousness a level higher than to the previous one. Consciousness that is associated with the higher level solves the problems of the lower.

Like the new moon that grows stage by stage and becomes a full moon, our mind grows stage by stage attaining maturity. Like the sun that bestows its light to earth at night, using moon as a medium, the "I" tenders its consciousness to the mind. As the reflected sun light through moon is entirely different in its intensity compared to the direct sun light, the reflected consciousness of the mind is entirely different from the "I" consciousness. The mind's consciousness expands and contracts in various contexts such as in fear, astonishment, ailments, tiredness, shock, bliss and so on. And also it is absent in deep-sleep and swoon. It is subjected to body's Constitution and its chemicals. But, the real "I" consciousness that is self-aware, exists as it is without any change and its awareness doesn't diminish under any circumstance. Even in deep-sleep, the "I" is aware of itself. For so long a time we only reside in the realms of mind and its growth in maturity. If we direct our awareness to "I" consciousness and start residing in it, it paves way for enlightenment. It is this enlightenment that burns the tree of ignorance and sorrow. To attain enlightenment, which death cannot touch, one has to just observe one's own face expressions and body movements and be with it. If one does so, the awareness that resided and focused only the mind, shifts to focussing the Self.

Chapter 4

Axle of the Wheel of Thoughts

According to the psychologists, a child is in the state of a complete "want;" It is in the want of food, protection, love, care, attention, praise, and so on. The child receives everything not only from its parents, but also from its relatives, neighbhours and unknown people as well. Wherever the child is taken, it is being surrounded and given attention, love, care and praise.

The child feels itself as the centre of attraction. It believes that the whole world is attending to it, taking care of it, praising it and thinking about it. The child feels completely protected in being the centre of attraction.

This conviction of "I am the centre of attraction" is deeply rooted in the tender mind of the child. To be the centre of attraction and thereby receive attention and love, the child sometimes even pretends to be in pain and sorrow. Since being in sorrow attracts more attention and care, the child develops the attitude of self-pity and unknowingly, suffering and sorrow becomes of high value in the deep recesses of the child's mind. Thereupon the entire structure of the child's psyche is formed by this 'being the centre of attraction.' While growing, this attitude with its delightful experiences of getting attention, love, protection, praise, and so on urges the mind to recur the experience. This particular form of desire becomes the base for various other desires. On the basis of this very desire, goals and achievements are being set up in one's mind, unknowingly perpetuating and strengthening childishness. Even the old aged people, unknowingly still carry this child mind throughout their life, by performing actions that attracts others towards them, in the hope of receiving love, care, attention, praise, etc.

Thus a human minds' sole requirement has become, that the whole world should surround and praise, applaud, attend and love it. If not the whole world, it expects at least one's town; if not the town, then at least a few. The body may grow older, but it is the child that is active inside that body throughout life.

This childhood behavior has positioned itself strongly in the "Receiving" end, i.e. want to receive love, attention, praise, and the like. Every activity that a human being does, every endeavor he embarks, every mission he wants to accomplish is urged by this deep-rooted attitude. One is completely unaware of the fact that one's psyche is imprisoned by this childhood mind. Maturity as we identify with age and experience exist only in the change of toys and not in the change of the very game. From childhood to adolescence, from adolescence to adulthood, the same old game with the same set of rules is being played; only the toys differ.

The sorrows, sufferings, pain, jealous, hatred, violence, sinful acts all are the outcome of this disposition of mind. Until this disposition of mind is transformed radically, one would lack real maturity, intelligence, peace and tranquility.

If one watches one's way of thoughts, every thought is a want of attention; every thought is a self-flattery.

In one's thought, one always talks to the other in such a way that the other praises him. Thoughts as such exist in this way. If one removes the axle of self-praise from the wheel of mind, the flow of recurring thoughts ceases instantaneously and the childishness with its fantasy is effaced, paving way for peace and Wisdom to be.

When this mind that has strengthened itself in the "receiving end," tenders love and attention to others, it tenders in the hope that it will receive the same back. If one removes the axle of self-flattery from the wheel of thoughts, one is freed from the life long imprisonment of childhood activity. Thereupon depression, frustration, disappointment, etc; ends, which were the inevitable consequences of Receiving ends' attitude. This liberated mind, for the first time, turns to the "Giving end," for it attains inexplicable peace. A human being who always acted with an expectation in mind, in his relationships, now gives love and affection for the sake of giving only. One whose mind is addicted to self-praise could tender true love, yet when they quell self-praise or self-attention from their thoughts, their minds are liberated from suffering, from where unconditional love is delivered.

A happy person is always at the "Giving" end, whereas an unhappy one is always at the "Receiving" end.

The real Love is a by-product of happiness. Usually the mind thinks that happiness is the outcome of love, whereas the reverse is the truth. Only a happy person can love. An unhappy person cannot love; it is the person who is peaceful and happy, capable of tendering love.

Happiness is a prerequisite for love to be; in turn, peace is a prerequisite for happiness to be; unwavering mind is a prerequisite for peace to be; further, cessation of self-praise is a prerequisite for an unwavering mind.

Hence, the level of one's self-praise determines the level of one's peace, happiness and love respectively.

Moreover, it is the level of love within oneself that determines one's way of thinking, motive, decisions and perspective. The way of one's thinking, motive, decisions and perspective is indeed one's intelligence. Therefore, the level of one's love is the level of their intelligence.

Chapter 5

The Mind and its control

Identification:

While watching a film in a television, one starts identifying oneself with a particular character and start experiencing vicariously. Since the television is at distance one can clearly distinguish oneself from it.

Like a television, our mind also runs a video in proximity, without distance between the onlooker and the video. Unknowingly, one fully identifies oneself with every video that the mind projects and experience accordingly. If one fully identifies oneself with thoughts, one becomes thoughts. As air becomes smell, one's awareness becomes to what it is associated and identified with.

There is an age long misconception that one becomes what he thinks. There revolves a theory that if one continuously think to achieve some position or goal in life, one would certainly achieve that position or goal through the power of that persistent thought. This theory, if pondered over genuinely without bias, has no fundamental reality in it. This great, mysterious life doesn't take its course according to one's narrow mind.

The statement "You become what you think" is completely different in dimension. It means, in the process of thinking, you become the thought. When dream happens in sleep, we forget that we are actually in bed, and completely identify with the dream and become that dream. In the same way, when thought happens, one identifies entirely with the thought and becomes that, without any distinction. In the thoughts of suffering, you become suffering; in the thoughts of joy, you become joy; in the thoughts of fear, you become fear. You become what you think.

Identification is a predominant characteristic of mind. It always identifies with one thing or the other and experience joy, sorrow or fear according to what it identifies with. Since mind can't help but identify, identification with the Real is advocated. When the mind identifies itself with the consciousness that is absolutely serene, the mind attains absolute serenity.

Myths and Sub-conscious:

A question always lingers as to why the ancient books of mythology and legends, although rich in its literature and ethics, written by the wise, contain some of the illogical, impossible and irrational incidences in their stories. Some are antagonistic about it, whereas others remain a common conventional believer. If one takes a dream scenario one could see all the illogical, irrational and complete impossibility happening in that dream. One even talks to the dead person in dream knowing fully well that they are no more.

Everyday dreams occur containing so many irrational events. Nobody including rationalists question the irrationalities while they dream, but conversely everybody believe those happenings as real. It is the same rational man who dreams, yet why couldn't he disregard and rebel against it while dreaming? Why does the inner mind displays irrationalities and impossibilities? Is a human being confined only to the upper layers of his mind or to the whole reach of his mind? The inner mind or sub-conscious mind is more powerful than the normal conscious mind. For a healthy mind, harmony between the sub-conscious and the conscious is necessary. Sub-conscious mind expects miracles and impossibilities to assuage itself. The irrationalities and miraculous scenes created in the myths are to address, assuage and balance one's sub-conscious mind, for the wise one's of the old knew that the sub-conscious is more powerful than the conscious. Further, the sub-conscious contrasts the outer mind's reasoning part. Hence, the creation of myths is to balance the contrasting logic and illogical parts of the same mind.

In the wakefulness state, we live not only with our conscious mind, but with the sub-conscious mind as well. The inner part of the mind which is termed as sub-conscious, instinctively craves for miracles, because it naturally possesses the power and energy to transform or get beyond our natural physical laws. All the discoveries and inventions of scientists are a bestowment of the sub-conscious. After all, mind is only partially subjected to this physical world; its very root does not belong to the physical realm.

Control of thoughts:

The thoughts either it be positive or negative is only a distraction to peace. To stop the unnecessary activities of the mind is not to slay the mind, but on the contrary, it is its enhancement. Since mind being the cause for experiences, the control over it for an enriched mundane experience is essential. Further, its stillness is necessary for spiritual experience.

Control of mind is gained by delaying a thought for two minutes. When a thought occurs in mind, one should postpone it for at least ten seconds initially. It is best if one suddenly stops a thought amidst activity, rather than allocating a specific time for this practice. Initially one should stop an occurring thought for ten seconds and then should allow it to recur. In the same manner, one should by and by increase the seconds gently up to two minutes and more. If one does it, one gains control over thoughts, reversing the usual process of thought controlling oneself.

A thought is composed of intelligence, unnecessary imagination, fear, sadness, hope etc.

In postponing and allowing it in another time, the intensity of negative part of thought will start vanishing, leaving the intelligent part intact. When the intensity of the negativities decrease, thoughts move slowly and peacefully. One could experience the fading away of fantasies and negativities of thoughts consciously in the wakeful state as well as sub-consciously in the dream state. If a sad thought or fearful thought is postponed for at least two minutes, it will not recur with the same intensity of sadness and fear as it occurred two minutes ago. Then once again, if one postpones it for another two minutes, then that particular thought will lose its strength to rise again in mind. One should begin this type of practice with one's normal thoughts initially, so that one will not stumble when controlling sad and fearful thoughts.

Stillness of mind:

The mind is in perpetual activity, except in deep-sleep and in swoon. The inexplicable bliss of deep-sleep is everybody's craving, since it ceases the 'experiencer' completely. To be fully aware of the absence of the "Experiencer" in the wakeful state is to bring forth the bliss of peace. The absence of thoughts is the absence of the 'Experiencer' and the presence of one's ever serene real "I am."

In the manner one happily renounced one's own "I" and entire thoughts that acted as a hindrance to deep-sleep, if one puts the right effort in the same manner and renounces one's entire thoughts in the wakeful state and attains stillness of mind, one realizes the ultimate truth that the sacred texts were trying to point out.

To drop the thoughts, one should precisely see the primary root of the tree of thoughts and cut it.

As humans we are always in relationship with other human beings. This 'other' is the possessor of our mind; this 'other' permeates the mind. The "Other" is the important particular of one's thought. If there were no "Other" in thought, one cannot think at all. The wheel of thought doesn't move without the 'other.' The tree of thought doesn't survive without the 'other.' Therefore, the 'other' is the primary root of the tree of thoughts.

There are three elements involved in thoughts. The "I," the "Other," the "Talking." If one stops any one of the elements from its occurrence, the other two drop away by themselves.

If one stops the occurrence of "I" in one's thought, i.e. imagining oneself in a particular posture, in a particular dress etc, the 'Other' and the 'Talking' are dropped automatically.

Or, if one deliberately stops imagining about the "Other," who may be a friend or a relative, then 'Talking' with them is stopped along with the "I" thought.

Or, if one stops the "Talking" i.e, one should not allow even one word to arise from the mind; then the "Other" along with the "I" thought is stopped.

Pictures and words form the mind. The thought of the "Other" and of the "I" are imaginary pictures, whereas "Talking" is in words. Pictures and words are intermingled and mutually triggers each other. If one stops any one element among the three by persistent effort, for at least three minutes, then they attain a great state of peace and bliss. The accumulated sins of the very long past, will start burning to ashes.

Chapter 6

The seer and the seen

A physicist who wants to discover the truth of origin and amazing operation of this universe is apparently part of this amazing universe. A person who sees the trees, flowers, the mountain, the valley, the stars, different types of creatures, and the like and astonished by the beauty of nature, belongs to that very nature.

The physicist who observes and analyses an object in the process of finding the real root and truth of this universe is not apart from the truth of the observed object, since the same truth lies both in the analyzer and the analyzed. Therefore, the observer and the observed are one in their core truth.

As an illustration, a poet and his poem can be separatively observed, similarly an artist and his art, a musician and his music, an author and his book can be distinctively observed; while a dance and the dancer cannot be separatively observed, as the beauty of the dance is inseparable from the dancer. Hence, observing the dance in itself is observing the dancer.

Similar to that, the whole of universe is a Sacred dance indistinguishable from the Sacred dancer. To see the dancer, one should see the dance. Since the observer is verily a part of the cosmic dance, he ought to be in self-observation to get attuned with the cosmic dancer. Since analysis of an outward object is done by senses, the truth found out will be within the limits of the senses only; it will not reveal the core truth that is operating the very senses itself. The known and the process of knowing are outcome of the senses. Therefore, that which is seen by eyes, that which is heard by ears, that which is felt, everything can never be the core of cores. In deep sleep senses are dormant. Our 'Being' is not an entity that belongs only to wakeful state. Our 'I' or 'Being' exist in deep-sleep state too. Since the core truth exist and operates even in deep-sleep while the senses are dormant, the research that is done in the wakeful state with the senses, can never reveal the absolute core truth that operates the very senses itself.

In deep-sleep, the observed as well as the observer are not present. While in waking, the observer always wakes with the observed. The observer is always inseparable from the observed. One's very 'Being' is independent of the 'observer' and the 'observed,' which is evident inferring deep-sleep. 'Observer' and 'observed' exist as a veil upon one's 'Being.'

Basically, what is a "Seeing?" When one sees a flower, the seer is the "I" and 'seen' is the flower.

The "I" sees a flower. In the process of seeing, where does the seer end and from where does the seen begin? Which is the demarcating line that separates the seer on one side and the seen on the other side? Where is the separation between the seer and the seen at the moment of seeing? There happens only "Seeing" without any separation between the seer and the seen.

As an illustration, a mirror reflects whatever comes in front of it. Mirror is always occupied with reflection. In no way a mirror can evade reflection. Similarly, the seer can never evade the seen. As a mirror, the seer reflects the seen. Here, a mirror has no memory, therefore it reflects only the present. Since human being as a seer has memories, he reflects the past 'seen' too. The seer is nothing but a constitution of past and present "Seen." Apart from this, if the seer has color blindness, he could see only black and white shades of that flower. Not only that, if the seer squints his eyes, he will see two flowers. The seen is a projection of one's eye and brain with its limitations. For an example, if some other person is bestowed with more power than a common man, he may see that flower perhaps entirely in a different colour and even in a different shape. For an understanding purpose, if we assume that a seer has deficiency in his brain in identifying shapes, then the flower as such is not seen at all. We are seeing an outward object with our brain or minds' perception that is already conditioned, defined and limited. It is the seer's brain or mind that gives color and a shape to the flower and perceives it as an object. The seer creates the seen. The seen is a projection of the seer. If there is no seer, then there is no seen either. Colour is projected on that flower by the seer. Shape is projected on that flower by the seer. That 'flower' is seen in that particular state because of the 'seer.' Therefore, the flower is a display of the seer. The trees, plants and the whole of universe seen is a projection of the mind as 'seer.' The seen comes from within the seer.

If in a mirror the reflecting layer is completely removed, the reflection ends. That substratum upon which this reflecting layer adhered to is the real core or origin of that mirror and its reflection. Similarly, the entity upon which our reflecting mind with its five senses is adhered to is the core and origin of us, as 'seer' and the universe seen. Deep-sleep is the only state where the seer and the seen is absent. Therefore, that which lives and exists in the deep-sleep of every living beings is the origin, center and core of this cosmos and all of its particulars. If a person, by following the right path, which suits his or her attitude and idiosyncrasy, accomplishes the cessation of the 'seer' and the 'seen' in one's conscious wakeful state, for a particular duration of time, then this core of cores is recognized.

Chapter 7

On Consciousness

Supposing you take up a journey to another town in a car, can you assert the movement of the car as your movement? It is the car that moves; not you. Due to the movement of the car we observe various scenarios.

Similarly, if you walk from one place to other, do you really move or does your body move? If your body stands upside down, does your "I am" become upside down? Does your awareness become upside down? Are you not the same in all positions of your body, such as sitting, standing, walking, running, spinning and the like? Are you not that 'Sameness' right from your childhood till your old age? Thoughts may change, perspective may change, body may grow, but the 'Sameness' persists. That 'Sameness' is nothing but serene Consciousness.

If one closes one's eyes and holds the breath for three or four seconds, and watches one's "I am" within, one would have a glimpse of one's real "I am" as serene consciousness. It is this serene consciousness that ever remains since one's childhood without any movement or change whatsoever.

By closing the eyes, one should stop the breath suddenly from its movement for three or four seconds either while inhaling or exhaling, and should watch one's "I am." While watching, one should hold on to that silent "I am" and leave the breath as usual. One should catch hold and be with that silent "I am." While being with that "I am," one would realize that it is profoundly silent and inexplicably alive consciousness and also it is not in a particular shape or form.

After having a glimpse of one's "I am" as serene consciousness and formless, one should also realize that it does not move even an inch. Only forms of some kind move from one place to other or gesticulate from one place. Also, only forms have an 'inside' to it. Since this serene consciousness that is self-aware, is beyond forms, it has no 'inside' to it. Since it has no 'inside,' it has also no 'outside' either. Since it exists without an inside and an outside, the whole 'Seen' is seemingly upon it, like a cinema that is projected upon a white screen. Since Consciousness has no inside and an outside, it is boundless without a beginning and an end; and immeasurable by any yardstick.

This serene consciousness is not within one's body, but the body exists upon it. From the stand point of the body, this Consciousness is within. From the stand point of this Consciousness, body is upon it. From the stand point of the projected cinema, the white screen is within it. From the stand point of the white screen, the whole of the pictures are upon it.

In a dream, one sees a tree at a distance, and walks towards and touches it. On waking up, one finds that the tree, the body, the space between them, the distance and time taken to reach the tree, the feeling of touching that tree everything to be the projection of his consciousness and that the same consciousness withdraws that entire space and objects within itself while waking from sleep. Similarly, all the physical bodies, space, objects, sun, the planets and the whole 'Seen,' of our wakeful state is the projection of one Super-Consciousness. Since everything is projection of consciousness, everything is consciousness. Since everything is consciousness, the consciousness is not dual; there is only one. This consciousness that exists as 'I' in everybody is one and same in everybody. Self-consciousness is same in everybody. "Self-consciousness" does not differ to each and every living beings.

Even as, emptiness is both within the house and without the house, Consciousness is both within and without the physical bodies and pervades everywhere. As the emptiness that is covered by four walls is called a house; the emptiness that is covered with a clay structure is called a pot, the Consciousness that is covered with a human body is called a human being; covered with an animal body is called an animal; likewise birds, insects, plants, trees, rocks, mountains, the sun and moon all are but this one consciousness.

In a human beings' body, the mind that exists in the head region while awake, in the throat region while dreaming and in the chest region while in deep-sleep is a bubble that is in control of the ocean of this Consciousness.

Chapter 8

Fate

A television set has many components in it such as picture tube, audio system, motherboard, receiver, exterior screen, and many other. A video is being telecasted through the television set from elsewhere. The video and audio become possible in the television due to proper functioning of all its inner parts. If a major part fails to function, the video is not manifested on the screen. Since the parts play a major role in the telecast, that does not in any way mean the parts relay the video on its own. They are mere a medium of relay. The video and the audio do not happen from the television set, but through the television set. The telecast is from somewhere outside the television.

One's heart, brain and all the organs of body are like parts of a television set. Thought and speech originates from elsewhere, using the organs of the body as a medium. Even though brain with its subtleties and control over the body seems to work by itself, yet it is the higher power that uses it as a tool.

Although there are innumerable physical bodies, yet all are one in their quality and nature. Colour, height and shape may differ, but it is the same. Any discovery in one physical body is the discovery of all the bodies. The invention of a medicine that cures one physical body, equally cures all the bodies. All bodies possess the same features. The nature of mind is also alike. In the way a person's mind thinks in fear, it is in the same way everybody's mind think. A billion unlit candle can take the flame from a single lit candle and may live separately on all sides of the globe, yet every flame of all the candles are one and the same. Similarly, consciousness that exists as "I am" in every physical bodies is only one. There are no multiple consciousness. Only one "I am" exists in many different bodies. We say somebody as the 'other;' but that other says himself as "I am" only. 'You,' 'He' are only terms for communication. All exist as "I" only. Everybody claims themselves as "I am" only. Just as, the feeling of a physical pain is same to everybody, the feeling of a joy is same to everybody, the feeling of "I" too is same to everybody. Therefore only one "I" expresses itself in every beings. This one "I" consciousness that exists within all the bodies, uses all the bodies and minds as a tool and performs all the happenings of the world. Since every action is impelled by this one "I" consciousness from within all the 'bodies,' even a tiny movement as well as moment to moment experience of every individual and creatures are predetermined and fixed. For an example, if a person meets his childhood friend unexpectedly in a public park, it is his "I" that impelled him to go to that park at that particular time. In the same way, it is his friends' "I" that has impelled him to go to that particular park at that particular time.

According to both their minds are concerned, this unexpected meeting is accidental. But, according to the "I" or Consciousness that exists behind both their minds, this occurrence is a fixed one. Only one "I" took both of them to that particular park at that particular time for the meeting to happen. Only our mind and body are separate and individualistic, not the very 'I.' Since we identify ourselves as 'I am,' only with our mind and body and not with our consciousness, we see ourselves as separate individuals. The individual mind is not thinking, but only receives thoughts. The iron nail may assume that it is moving on its own accord, but it is the powerful magnet that pulls it. Therefore, the movement of iron nail has its supply of force from the invisible energy of the magnet. Each and every second, by urging every living beings' mind and body to a particular action, it is this one "I" that performs all the occurrences of the world.

Since consciousness is only one, there is no second entity apart from consciousness to make the world occurrences accidental. This being the actuality, the whole happenings of the world among human beings and among other creatures is concretely predetermined. This consciousness does not exist with the feeling "I am." Because, to say "I am," the 'other' is needed. Since the 'other' is also this very same "consciousness," to whom will it assert itself as "I am?" Consciousness is beyond duality of 'I' and 'you.'

The shape, height, design and all other features and qualities of a tree is already imprinted in the seed. The seed that grows, attain only its predetermined state. The tree is incapable of deviating from its destined design. The seed merely unfolds its predetermined design at every moment of its growth. All of the creatures and every human being and their lives are designed beforehand and the existence merely unfolds it like a seed every moment.

Once a sage went on a visit to other village along with ten of his disciples, to collect some herbs. They passed through a forest to reach the village sooner. While walking in the forest, they saw a small pretty plant with a few tender leaves alongside. One of the disciples who always create an argument with the Sage, stopped near that plant and asked the Sage whether that pretty plant will grow as a big tree and survive for years. The Sage stood near the plant with closed eyes for a few minutes and replied, "Yes, this plant is destined to grow into a big tree and live for long years." Instantly after the Sage's reply, the disciple plucked that plant from the root and threw it away. He laughed at it and said, "Now Master! Look I proved you wrong. The plant's destiny which you saw in your vision, was only your imagination. There is no destiny for anybody. Everything is accidental."

The Sage uttered no word and continued his walking. That disciple boasted his win over the master among other disciples and enjoyed talking about it. At dusk, they reached the other village and stayed at an ashram (a religious retreat.) Suddenly there started a heavy rain that continued the whole night. Two days later after collecting enough herbs, the Sage with his disciples returned to their hometown through the same forest. When they arrived near the place where the plant was plucked and thrown away, every disciple was awe-struck to see the same plant that was thrown away got firmly rooted in the soil and sprang with new leaves. They realized that the heavy downpour of that night, pushed the plant's root inside of the soil and gave back its life.

The disciple who plucked that plant fell at the Sage's feet and begged for forgiveness of his ignorance. The Sage with a benign smile replied, "Everybody and everything move in accord only with the destined course. If anything deviates from the destined course by any hindrance, then miracles happen to restore the order again."

Chapter 9

Renunciation

Once there lived a king who always revered hermits and saints. Whenever he came to know that a saint lived somewhere, even if it's in another kingdom, he would immediately visit the sage, considering it a pilgrimage and would listen to his discourse with great fervor.

One day he came to know that a Saint in a loin cloth was staying in a temple in his own kingdom. In an overwhelming joy, the king went to visit the sage, along with the queen and ministers. In the temple, he saw the sage sitting quietly with closed eyes and spine upright. The king was patiently waiting for the sage to open his eyes. When the sage opened his eyes, the king bowed humbly before him with folded hands and beseeched him to visit his palace and stay with him for a few days, so that he would listen to his spiritual instructions.

Without any slight hesitation the Sage instantly agreed and got ready to go with the king. The king was bewildered a little. He didn't expect the saint's immediate assent to live with him in the palace. Anyhow, he was quite happy and took him to his palace. The king provided him a beautiful room with a cushion bed, and also offered nicely woven silk clothes and lot of gold ornaments to wear. The Saint accepted everything without any hesitation and wore them all. The king was astonished, for he believed that the saint would ignore these offers of gold and silk.

A suspicion has started to creep on king's mind as to whether this man is really a hermit who has renounced the earthly pleasures or is pretending to be one.

A few days passed the same way, and the king's suspicion has started growing day by day as the saint seems to be enjoying all the comforts of the palace. Also whenever the king starts a conversation about spiritualism the saint would always ignore the conversation.

The queen and the ministers advised the king to send this man out of palace, as he seems to be a posturer. Gathering courage, the king approached the saint and reluctantly expressed his state of mind that made him suspicious regarding his sainthood and stood for clarification.

In a gentle tone the saint replied "My dear King! You are an earnest aspirant and you ought to know the real meaning of Renunciation." On saying so, the saint removed all the gold ornaments and the silk cloth he was wearing, and sat in a loin-cloth as before without losing his serene mind. He explained to the king that possessing gold and richness, and losing the same would not in any way affect his serenity and equipoise of mind. The saint continued, "Though I was wearing gold and living with the richness that you offered, yet I was not attached to any of it even a bit. Since I have found the eternal bliss within, which is not dependent on any outward things, 'whatever is' or 'whatever is not' outside of me, do not affect me. Dear King, human mind possesses outward things that are impermanent to gain happiness. At the same time it is gripped with fear of losing the same. Due to fear, attachment on things grow stronger, that eventually leads to more fear. Human mind gets caught in this vicious circle. A fearful mind is not in peace. On realizing that it is the attachment on impermanent things that distracts peace, a sincere human mind finds ways and means to renounce attachments. After putting strenuous effort, that sincere mind is shown that renunciation is not an act of will or a state attained through effort, but it is a 'consequence.' That earnest mind is shown that attachment on that which is permanent and eternal, automatically and effortlessly ceases the attachments on impermanent things. Then, after proper investigation and insight, that sincere mind realizes that it is his own 'I' within, which is alive even in deep-sleep, is that permanent and eternal entity. After many attempts, the mind at last finds a suitable way to hold the 'I' firmly, without any distraction of thoughts. Even as, a river becomes the ocean while touching ocean, the mind becomes pure consciousness by holding on to the 'I,' and dwells in inexplicable peace. As a result of tasting the everlasting bliss of that inexplicable peace, attachment on outward things ceases automatically and effortlessly and renunciation ensues." The king genuflected with tears of gratitude and for the first time in his life has experienced a profound silence. The King beseeched the saint for further enlightenment.

Saint: If a person sincerely questions, what is this cosmos? What is this life all about? Where was I before my birth? How did I suddenly came into existence? Where did I go in deep sleep? Who am I? Where does this "I" reside in the body? Is there really a God? he starts searching for the answer sincerely. To those who truthfully yearns for it, the supreme Lord reveals his presence to the aspirant at the right time and through right method bestows a taste of enlightenment beforehand and shows the right path for him to follow. From then on the aspirant takes up his journey of enlightenment with the guidance of the supreme Lord.

King: All scriptures ascertain that the destruction of thoughts is the way for emancipation. Does that mean to destruct even the good thoughts?

Saint: A man went to other town for his business deals and was returning home after making a good profit. He had earned a lot of money and gold out of his business. On his way home, he was suddenly abducted by three thieves into a dense forest. After snatching away all of his belongings, the first-thief drew a sharp knife from his waist to kill the man. The other two thieves stopped the first-thief by saying that it was unnecessary to kill him as they had already taken away all of his possessions. But the first-thief refuted that if he were left alive he would apprise the people of town. The second-thief argued, in that case we would tie him up in a tree so that he could not move. The other two agreed and eventually, the man was tied up in a tree and the three thieves had left the place. The whole place was surrounded by darkness and the man screamed aloud for help as he was put up in great distress. He tried too hard to untie himself, but all of his efforts went in vain. Hours passed in fear and pain. After losing all his hopes, suddenly to his astonishment, the third-thief appeared before him. He freed the man from entanglement and asked him to go home.

The astounded man thanked the thief profusely, and humbly asked him to show the way to get out of the dense forest, as he had no idea about the way out. The thief agreed and held the man's hand and started walking in the maze of forest. After long hours of silent walking the thief showed the main road that connects the man's hometown. In a kind voice the thief said to him, "Follow this path, now this is your way to home!"

The man thankfully hugged the thief with tears and humbly invited him as a guest of honour to his home, to have a dinner at his parlor as a token of his love and gratitude. The thief held the man's hand

and said "Sir, I understand your concern and also understand your honest invitation to your home. Although I have helped you in finding out your way to home, yet I have no right or authority to enter even your town, for I am a thief, anyhow."

Here, the man is the Soul. The three thieves are three tendencies of the mind namely *tamas*, *rajas* and *sattva*. *Tamas* being greedy, envious, and which possesses destructive thoughts, tried to kill the Soul; *Rajas* being active, intelligent, ambitious, dominant, and yet swirl in confusion and suspicion, imprisons the Soul permanently; *Sattva* being good, constructive, humble, empathetic and intuitive shows the path to one's home. The dense forest is *Maya* or ignorance. The belongings of the man are one's *Karma (effects of previous action.)* After the three *gunas* or tendencies snatch all the *Karmas* of a person, it is the *Sattva* that shows the way for one's home, which is liberation. Even though *Sattva* has helped in showing the way, it has no rights to stay with the Soul, for *Sattva* too belongs to the forest of ignorance.

King: To attain enlightenment and deliverance, if one has to experience the consequences of all his previous actions and become free of karmas, how could one ever overcome the endless ebb and flow of the tide of one's 'Action?'

Saint: Realizing very clearly that one is not the 'Doer' of anything but only the supreme Lord is, puts an end to the ignorance that "I am the Doer," thereby ending one's *Karmas*.

King: What is the cause of our feeling that we are the 'Doer,' when really the supreme Lord is?

Saint: Ignorance due to absolute inattention to our own thoughts and action.

King: How to get rid of this ignorance?

Saint: To hold and be in union with the Supreme Lord is the path to eradicate ignorance.

King: How can I hold and be in union with the Supreme Lord?

Saint: Since all of the body's action is done only by the Supreme Lord, simply waiting and watching as to how the Supreme Lord within, is going to move your body the very next moment, is to hold and be in union with the Supreme Lord.

King: What happens to a person who is in union with the Lord, thus?

Saint: The door of deliverance opens at the appropriate time.

King: What does one encounter when that door opens?

Saint: The Holy Truth...

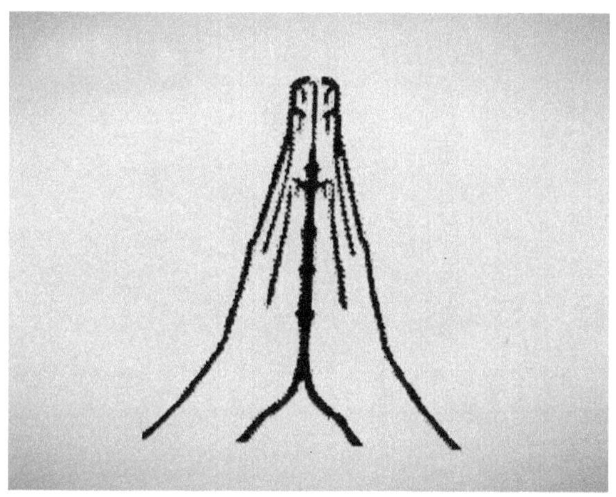

ஞானத்தின் சுவை

பொருளடக்கம்

முன்னுரை 77

1. மெய் நிலை 81
2. “அனுபவிப்பவர்” யார்? 95
3. முதிர்ச்சியும் ஞானமும் 104
4. எண்ண சக்கரத்தின் அச்சாணி 110
5. மனமும் அதன் கட்டுப்பாடும் 117
6. பார்ப்பவரும், பார்க்கப்படுவதும் 129
7. தன்னுணர்வு 138
8. விதி 145
9. துறவு 155

முன்னுரை

இந்தப் புத்தகம் ஆன்மீகத்தை பற்றியும், உயிரினங்களின் அடிப்படை உண்மையைப் பற்றியும் எடுத்துரைக்க முயல்கிறது. ஒரு மனிதர், தனது அனைத்து சூழ்நிலைகளிலும், நிலைகளிலும் சிந்தித்த வண்ணமே உள்ளார். அனைத்து தருணங்களிலும் சிந்தனை அவசியமாகிறது என்ற காரணத்தினால் அல்ல, ஆனால் சிந்திக்கும் பழக்கத்திற்கு ஒருவர் அடிமையாகிவிட்ட காரணத்தினால் என்பதனை இப்புத்தகம் மேற்கோள் காட்டுவதோடு, மனதின் உண்மைத் தன்மையை தெளிவாக தெரிந்து கொள்ளுதல், ஒருவரை மாயை மற்றும் அளவில்லா எண்ண ஓட்டங்களின் பிடியில் இருந்து மீட்டெடுத்து, அமைதிக்கு வழி வகுக்கிறது என்பதனை சுட்டிக் காட்டுகிறது. இந்தப் புத்தகத்தை எழுதுபவர், இறை உண்மையை அனுபவித்ததின் நிலைப்பாட்டில் இருந்து இவற்றை எழுதலாகிறார். இப்புத்தகம், பேருண்மையிடத்தில் சரணாகதி அடையும் வழியை முன்மொழிகிறது.

எழுதுபவர்,

மகேஷ்.

இப்பொழுது,

அந்த புனிதத்தின் பெயரால்;

அந்த பேருண்மையின் பெயரால்;

அந்த நித்திய பரமாத்மாவின் பெயரால்;

“சத்தியத்துடன் சங்கமித்தல்”
விவரிக்கப்படுகிறது.

1

மெய் நிலை

வெகுகாலமாய், மனிதர்கள், தன்னை விட மிகப் பெரிய சக்தி ஒன்று இருப்பதாகவும், அதுவே அனைத்தையும் படைத்து அனைவரையும் அவரவர் விதிக்கு ஏற்றார்போல் நடத்திச் செல்கிறது எனவும் நம்பிக்கை கொண்டுள்ளனர். மேலும் வேறு சிலர் இந்த நம்பிக்கை அற்றவர்களாக விளங்குகின்றனர்.

உயர் சக்தி ஒன்று உண்டு என்ற நம்பிக்கை உள்ளவர்கள் மற்றும் அந்த நம்பிக்கை இல்லாதோர் இரு வகையினருமே, தமது வாழ்வு தம் "தேர்வின்" படி தான் நகர்கிறது அல்லது தமது வாழ்வு தம் கையில்தான் உள்ளது என்ற திடமான நம்பிக்கையும் கொண்டுள்ளனர்.

ஒருவர், தான் சிந்திப்பதும் செயலாற்றுவதும் தன்னுடைய சுய தேர்வு மற்றும் விருப்பத்தின் படியே என்ற திட நம்பிக்கையோடே உள்ளார். இந்த நம்பிக்கை அசைக்க முடியாதவாறும், இதற்கு எதிரான விரித்துரைத்தலை மறுத்து ஒதுக்கும்படியாகவுமே ஒருவரின் நிலைப்பாடு உள்ளது.

நம் வாழ்வு, நம் சுய விருப்பம் அல்லது தேர்வின் படி நகர்கின்றதா அல்லது தன்நிகழ்வாக தாமாகவே நகர்கின்றதா? உயர் சக்தி என ஒன்று உண்டா இல்லையா என்பதை தெளிவாக உணர, வெறும் மேலோட்ட "நம்பிக்கை" என்பது போதுமானதாக இராது. மிக உன்னிப்பான, மனமார்ந்த மற்றும் உண்மையான ஆய்வு, பேருண்மையை வெளி கொணர தேவைப்படுகிறது. நமது எண்ணங்களும் செயல்களும் நமது விருப்பம் படியே அல்லது நமது தேர்வின் படியே உள்ளது என்ற மனிதனின் நம்பிக்கையானது, பலவிதமான தத்துவங்களை, பல்வேறு விதமான மனிதர்களால், பல்வேறு காலகட்டத்தில் படைக்கப்பட்டு, அவை பல்வேறு குழுக்களாகவும் பிரிவுகளாகவும் அமைந்து இயங்குகின்றது. இவ்வனைத்து தத்துவங்கள் மற்றும் கோட்பாடுகளும் "மனிதன் சுயமாக செயல் படுகிறான்" என்ற சித்தாந்தத்தை அடிப்படையாக கொண்டுள்ளமையால், ஒரு மனிதரிடமிருந்து வெளிப்படும் "செயல்" எனப்படுவதை, மிகத் தெளிவாகவும் முழுமையாகவும் ஆய்வு செய்ய வேண்டியது அத்தியாவசியமான ஒன்றாக விளங்குகிறது.

"செயல்" என்கின்ற வார்த்தை "அசைவு" என்பதனை சுட்டிக் காட்டுகிறது. உடல் மற்றும் மனதின் அசைவு ஆகும் அவை. உடல் மற்றும்

மனதின் அசைவுகளை கவனிப்பது என்பது "செயலின்" உண்மைத் தன்மையை கவனித்தல் என்பதாகும். உட்காருதல், நடத்தல், கைகளை உயர்த்துதல், தலையை திருப்புதல் போன்ற உடலின் பல்வேறு அசைவுகள் அல்லது செயல்பாடுகள், ஒருவரின் விருப்பத்தினாலும் சுய தேர்வினாலும் நடைபெறுகிறது என ஒருவரால் நம்பப்படுகிறது. ஆனால், ஒருவர் உற்று நோக்கினால், உடலானது செயல்புரிய சுவாசம், இரத்தஓட்டம்மற்றும்அனைத்துஉள்உறுப்புகளின் செயற்படும் ஆற்றல், அத்தியாவசியமாகிறது. சுவாசத்தை ஒருவர் கவனிப்பாரேயானால் சுவாசமானது, தன்னிச்சையாக தாமே நிகழ்ந்து கொண்டிருப்பதே அன்றி, அது ஒருவரின் "செயல்" அல்ல. இதே போன்று, இரத்த சுழற்சியும் மற்றும் ஒவ்வொரு உள் உறுப்புகளின் செயற்பாடுகளும், தன்நிகழ்வாக தாமாகவே செயல்பட்டுக் கொண்டிருக்கின்றனவே அன்றி இவை எவையும் ஒரு மனிதன் "நான் செய்கிறேன்" என்று கூறும் வகையிலான செயல்கள் அல்ல.

தன்நிகழ்வாக தாமாகவே இயங்கும் இந்த சுவாசம், இரத்த ஓட்டம் மற்றும் உள் உறுப்புகளின் துணை இல்லாமல், ஒருவரால் நடப்பது, உட்காருவது, கைகளை அசைப்பது, தலையை திருப்பி பார்ப்பது போன்ற செயல்களை

செய்ய இயலாது. எனவே, இவ்வுடல் நடப்பதும் அசைவதும் எனது இச்சைக்கு ஏற்பவே என ஒருவர் நம்புவதற்கு பின்புலத்தில், தன்னை மீறிய மிக உயர்ந்த சக்தி ஒன்று இவ்வுடலை ஆட்கொண்டு இயக்கிக் கொண்டிருக்கிறது என்பது புலப்படுகிறது.

எந்த உயர் சக்தி இவ்வுடலில் மூச்சை இயக்குகிறதோ, அதே உயர் சக்தி தான் இவ்வுடலின் மிக மேலோட்டமான சிறு விரல் அசைவுகளுக்கும் காரணமே அன்றி நாம் இல்லை.

செயலின் உண்மை :

நீங்கள் சிறு குழந்தையாக இருக்கும்பொழுது "நான்" என்ற தனிப்பட்ட அடையாளம் உங்களுக்கு இருக்கவில்லை. உங்களின் சுவாசம், கைகள், கால்கள், கண்கள், தலை அனைத்தும் தாமாகவே அசைந்து செயல்பட்டது.

உங்கள் உடலின் எந்த பாகத்தையும் நீங்கள் செயல்பட வைக்கவில்லை. தாமாகவே சுவாசம் செய்து, ஜீரணம் செய்து, கழிவுகளை வெளியேற்றி, வியர்வை சிந்தி, கை கால்களை அசைத்து, உறங்கி மற்றும் விழித்து செயல் புரிந்த அதே உடலானது வளர ஆரம்பிக்கிறது. சிறிது காலத்திற்குப் பின் "நான்" என்ற ஒரு தனிப்பட்ட அடையாளம் நிலைகொள்ள ஆரம்பிக்கிறது. "நான்" என்ற அந்த அடையாளத்தை அடைந்த பிறகு, ஏற்கனவே தன்நிகழ்வாக தாமாகவே சுவாசம் செய்து, ஜீரணம் செய்து, கழிவுகளை வெளியேற்றி, வியர்வை சிந்தி, கை கால்களை அசைத்து, உறங்கி மற்றும்

விழித்து இயல்பாக இயங்கிக் கொண்டிருந்த அந்த உடலோடு இந்த “நான்” என உதித்தது, தன்னை அதனுடன் ஒப்பிட்டு அடையாளப் படுத்திக் கொள்கிறது. இதன் விளைவாக, தாமாகவே சீராக இயங்கும் அந்த உடலின் செயற்பாட்டினை, “எனது” செயற்பாடு என அந்த “நான்” அடையாளப் படுத்திக் கொள்கிறது. உங்கள் தலை தாமாக திரும்பினால், “நான் தான்” திருப்பினேன் என நம்புகிறீர்கள். உங்கள் கை எதையாவது எடுத்தால் “நீங்கள்” எடுப்பதாக நம்புகிறீர்கள். அந்த உடல் அதனை தற்காத்துக் கொள்ள எதனை நோக்கியாவது அச்சம் கொண்டால், “நீங்கள்” அஞ்சுவதாக நம்புகிறீர்கள். ஆனால் உண்மையில், எந்த உயர் சக்தி நீங்கள் சிறு குழந்தையாக இருந்தபொழுது உங்களின் அனுமதியின்றி உங்களுள் மூச்சு விட்டுக் கொண்டிருந்ததோ, கை கால்களை அசைத்ததோ, அழுததோ, சிரித்ததோ, அதே உயர் சக்தி தான் இப்பொழுதும் கூட உங்கள் உடலில் செயல் புரிபவராக திகழ்கிறது. நீங்கள் எந்த நேரத்திலும் அந்த உயர் சக்தியை வெற்றிகொண்டு உடலின் செயற்பாட்டினை உங்களின் கட்டுப்பாட்டிற்குள் கொண்டுவரவுமில்லை, அல்லது எந்த ஒரு தருணத்திலும் அந்த உயர் சக்தி, உடலை இயக்கி செயல் புரியும் தனது அதிகாரத்தை உங்களுக்கு விட்டுக் கொடுக்கவும் இல்லை.

இருந்தபோதிலும், நான் தான் என் உடலை அசைத்து இயக்குகிறேன் என்ற அசைக்க முடியாத உணர்வு ஒருவர்க்கு எதனால் ஏற்படுகிறது? அதன் காரணம் என்னவெனில், உங்கள் கைகள் எதையாவது எடுப்பதற்கு முன்னால், அந்தப் பொருளை எடுக்க வேண்டும் என்ற எண்ணம் உங்களுக்குள் எழுகிறது. உங்கள் உடல் ஒரு செயலைச் செய்வதற்கு சற்று முன்னதாக அந்தச் செயலுக்கு உண்டான எண்ணம் உங்கள் மனதில் எழுகிறது. நீங்கள் சிறு குழந்தையாக இருந்தபொழுது அதே கைகள் எண்ணங்களின்றி ஒரு பொருளைப் பற்றியது. ஆனால் இப்பொழுது அதே கைகள் மனதின் ஒரு எண்ணத்தை பின்பற்றி பற்றுகிறது. உங்களுள் எழும் எண்ணங்களை, “உங்களுடைய” எண்ணங்கள் என்று நீங்கள் அடையாளங் கண்டுகொண்டுள்ளமையால், இவ்வுடலை அசைத்து செயல் புரிவது நீங்கள் தான் என திடமாக நம்புகிறீர்கள். எண்ணங்களின் ஆதாரம் எது? எங்கிருந்து, எவ்வாறு அது எழுகிறது? எண்ணங்கள் உண்மையில் ஒருவரின் கட்டுப்பாட்டிற்குள், ஒருவரின் சொந்த விருப்பத்திற்கு உட்பட்டு உள்ளனவா அல்லது “எண்ணங்கள்,” தன்நிகழ்வாக தாமாகவே ஒருவருள் எழுகின்றனவா? நான் எனது சுய நினைவோடு, எனது விருப்பத்தின் படி தான் சிந்திக்கிறேன் என

ஒருவர் நம்பினால், பிறகு ஏன் எண்ணங்களை ஒருவரால் கட்டுப்படுத்த முடியவில்லை? எண்ணங்கள் நமது கட்டுப்பாட்டில் உள்ளதா அல்லது எண்ணங்களின் கட்டுப்பாட்டில் நாம் இருக்கிறோமா? எண்ணங்கள் எனது சுய தேர்வு அல்லது எனது விருப்பம் போல் எழுகின்றன என்ற நம்பிக்கை, கானல் நீரைப் போன்று வெறும் மாயத் தோற்றம் ஆகும். ஒருவர் மிக உன்னிப்புடன் தம்முள் நிகழ்வதை கவனித்தால், ஒரு எண்ணமானது நமது கவனத்திற்கு முந்தையதாகவே தோன்றுகிறது என்பதனை தெளிவாக அறிந்து கொள்ள இயலும். தன்நிகழ்வாக தாமாகவே ஒரு எண்ணம் நம்முள் தோன்றிய பிறகு தான், நமது கவனம் அதன்மீது விழுகின்றது. ஒரு எண்ணம் தாமாகவே தோன்றிய பின்பு தான் நாம் அதை கவனிக்கின்றோம். ஒரு எண்ணம் தாமாகவே நம் மனதில் தோன்றி ஒரு விநாடிக்கும் குறைந்த கால அளவிற்குப் பிற்பாடுதான் நமது விழிப்புணர்வும் கவனமும் அந்த எண்ணத்தின் மீது விழுகிறது. தாமாகவே எழும் எண்ணங்களும் அதன் பிற்பாடு அதன் மீது விழும் நமது விழிப்புணர்வும் மிக வேகமாக நடைபெறுவதால், நாம் நமது விழிப்புணர்வோடு சிந்திப்பதாக அனுமானம் செய்து கொள்கிறோம். நான் தான் சுயமாக சிந்திக்கிறேன் என்ற நம்பிக்கை, உள்ளே நிகழும் இத்தகைய வேகமான நிகழ்வால் ஏற்படுகிறது. “நான்” என்ற ஒருவரின்

தன்னுணர்வானது, தாமாகவே எழும் எண்ணங்கள் மற்றும் தாமாகவே அசையும் உடல் இவைகளுக்கு இடையே வாசம் செய்து கொண்டிருக்கிறது. எந்த உயர் சக்தியின் ஆற்றலினாலும் பீடிப்பினாலும் உடலின் அசைவுகள் மற்றும் செயல்பாடுகள் இயங்குகின்றதோ, அதே உயர் சக்தியில் இருந்து தான் அனைத்து எண்ணங்களும் தோன்றுகிறது. "நான்" என்பது பரிசுத்தமான விழிப்பு நிலை மட்டுமே ஆகும். உதாரணத்திற்கு, ஒரு பாத்திரம் என்பது யாது? பாத்திரம் என்பது உண்மையில் அதன் வடிவமா அல்லது அந்த வடிவத்தினுள் இருக்கும் வெற்றிடமா? ஒரு பானையில் நீர் நிரப்பப்பட்டால் அந்த நீரானது உண்மையில் எங்கு நிரப்பப்படுகிறது? அது அந்த பானையினுள் இருக்கும் வெற்றிடத்தில் தானே நிரம்புகிறது?

எனவே, பானை என்றால் வெற்றிடம் என்பதே நிதர்சனமான உண்மை. அந்த வெற்றிடத்தைச் சுற்றி களிமண்ணால் செய்த கட்டமைப்பு, நீரானது கீழே விழாமல் பார்த்துக்கொள்ள ஏற்பாடு செய்த ஒரு பாதுகாப்பு அறணே ஆகும். வெற்றிடத்தைச் சுற்றி அமைக்கப்பட்டிருக்கும் பல்வேறு வடிவிலான கட்டமைப்பை, நாம் பல்வேறு பெயர் சூட்டி அழைக்கின்றோம். சிலவற்றை பானை என்றும், சிலவற்றை கூடை என்றும், வாகனம் என்றும், வீடு என்றும், பறவைகளின் கூடு என்றும், வெற்றிடத்தை, அதனை சுற்றி இருக்கும் அரணின் வடிவமைப்பை வைத்து அழைக்கின்றோம். வெற்றிடமே அனைத்திற்கும் ஆதாரம் ஆகும். அதுபோன்றே, உடலால் சூழப்பட்ட, எண்ணங்களால் நிரப்பப்பட்ட ஒருவரின் உண்மையான "நான்" எனப்படுவது பகுத்து அறிய முடியாத, பிரித்தறிய இயலாத மாபெரும் விழிப்பு நிலை ஆகும்.

தற்போது நாம் அடையாளப் படுத்திக் கொள்கிற "நான்" எனப்படுவது யாது? உதாரணத்திற்கு, ஒருவரின் அனைத்து ஞாபகங்களையும் ஏதாவது ஒரு மின் சக்தியின் மூலமோ அல்லது வேறு வழியிலோ மூளையில் இருந்து அகற்றிவிட்டால், அந்த குறிப்பிட்ட நபர் எவ்வாறு நடந்து கொள்வார்? அவரால்,

தான் யார் என்று அடையாளங் கண்டு கொள்ள இயலுமா? அவருக்கு, இதற்கு முன்னதாக இருந்த "நான்" என்பது இப்போது இல்லை. ஆக, இந்நிலையில் துல்லியமாக, "நான்" என்பது யாது? ஒருவரின் "நான்" என்பது அவரின் ஞாபகங்களே. எண்ணங்களால் ஆன ஞாபகங்கள் அழிக்கப்பட்டு விட்டால் தற்போது அடையாளப் படுத்திக்கொள்ளப்படும் "நான்" என்பதும் அத்துடனே அழிக்கப்பட்டுவிடுகிறது. நீங்கள் சிறு குழந்தையாக இருந்தபொழுது, எண்ணங்களோ அல்லது ஞாபகங்களோ இல்லாமல் முழுவதுமாக, நிகழும் இந்த கணத்தில் இருந்தீர்கள். அப்பொழுது எண்ணங்கள் உங்களை ஆட்கொள்ளவில்லை. எனவேதான் உங்களால் உங்களைச் சுற்றியிருந்த சிற்சிறு விவரங்களையும் கூட கூரிய கவனத்துடன் கிரகிக்க முடிந்தது. நீங்கள், "இதுவே நான்" என்ற தனிப்பட்ட ஒரு அடையாளமின்றி வாழ்ந்தீர்கள். காலப்போக்கில், நடக்கும் நிகழ்வுகள் உங்கள் மூளையில் ஞாபகங்களாக பதிய ஆரம்பித்தன. அந்த ஞாபகங்கள், எண்ணங்களாக உருவெடுத்து தோன்றுகையில், உங்களுக்கு "சென்ற காலம்" என ஒன்று உண்டானது. "சென்ற காலம்" என்ற அந்த நினைவுகளின் கூடவே "நான்" என்ற ஒரு தனி அடையாளமும் வந்து சேர்ந்தது. சென்ற காலத்தின் நீக்கம், "நான்" என்பதன்

நீக்கம் ஆகும். நினைவுகளின் அகற்றம், "நான்" என்பதன் அகற்றமாகும். ஆகவே, "நான்" என்பது "எண்ணங்கள்" அல்லது "சென்ற காலம்" அன்றி வேறில்லை. இந்த "எண்ணங்கள்" உருவாக்கிய "நான்" என்பது 'கற்பனை' மற்றும், தேடினால் புலப்படாத மாயையானது. இந்த "எண்ணங்கள்" உருவாக்கிய "நான்," உண்மையான "நான்"ஆக விளங்கும் விழிப்பு நிலையை மறைக்கும் திரையாக செயல்படுகிறது. சென்ற காலம் உருவாக்கிய இந்த "நான்"ஐ நீக்குவோர், எப்பொழுதும் இந்த கணத்தில் மட்டுமே வசிக்கும் உண்மையான "நான்" என்பதின் புனித தரிசனத்தை பெறுகின்றனர். மாயை "நான்" என்பதன் வேர், சென்ற காலத்திலும், உண்மையான "நான்" என்பதன் வேர், என்றென்றும் இந்த கணத்திலும் நிலை கொண்டுள்ளது.

இந்த மாயை "நான்"ஐ நீக்கி, உண்மையான "நான்"இன் தரிசனம் பெற ஒருவர் விழைவாரேயானால், அவர் தன்னைத்தானே, அடுத்தவரை கவனிப்பதைப் போல கவனித்தல் வேண்டும். நாம் வழக்கமாக அடுத்தவரை எவ்வாறு கவனிப்போம்? நாம் அடுத்தவரின் முக பாவனைகளையும் உடல் அசைவுகளையும் அல்லவா கவனிப்போம்? துல்லியமாக அதுபோலவே, ஒருவர் தன்னுடைய முக

பாவனைகள் மற்றும் உடல் அசைவுகளை கவனித்தல் வேண்டும். மகிழ்ச்சி, சோகம், ஏக்கம், ஆச்சரியம், பயம், கோபம், விரக்தி, சிரிப்பு போன்ற எந்த ஒரு அனுபவத்தின் போதும் ஒருவர் தன்னுடைய முகம் எவ்வாறு ஒரு அனுபவம் நிகழும்போது தாமாக பாவனை செய்கிறது, தம் உடல் எவ்வாறு அவ்வனுபவத்தின் போது தாமாக அசைகிறது என வெறுமனே கவனிக்க வேண்டும். குறிப்பாக கண்கள், உதடு, நாக்கு மற்றும் கை விரல்கள் எவ்வாறு பாவனை செய்கிறது என்பதனை கவனிக்க வேண்டும். இவ்வகை கவனம் சில நிமிடங்கள் தொடர வேண்டும். இவ்வாறு கவனிக்கும் பொழுது, உங்களின் முக பாவனை மற்றும் உடல், அசைவின்றி சிறிது நேரம் விளங்கும். அந்த அசைவின்மைமேல் உங்கள் கவனம் தொடர வேண்டும். அந்த அசைவின்மையோடு உங்கள் கவனம் ஒத்திசைவோடு இருப்பது என்பது ஒப்புயர்வற்ற உயர் சக்தியுடன் ஒன்றுகூடி இருப்பதாகும். ஒரு ஜீவனின் இந்த தூய செயலானது, வார்த்தைகளுக்கு அப்பாற்பட்டது. இருப்பினும், இதற்கு ஓர் பெயர் சூட்டி அடையாளப் படுத்திக் கொள்ள வேண்டும் எனில், இதுவே “சத்சங்கம்” ஆகும். “சத்” என்றால் உண்மை அல்லது சத்தியம்; “சங்கம்” என்றால் ஒன்றிணைவது. சத்சங்கம் என்றால் ஆற்றல்

பெற்ற பேருண்மையுடன் ஒன்றுகலப்பது. அந்நிலையில், என்றும் புதியதாய் விளங்கும், காலத்திற்கும் தூரத்திற்கும் அப்பாற்பட்ட, ஆனந்த புன்னகைபடைத்த “அவர்” உங்களை ஆட்கொண்டு, செயல் அனைத்தையும் புரிவது தாமே என உணர்த்துகிறார். அந்த கணத்தில், சத்தியத்தை உணர்ந்த ஜீவன், தன்னையே பரிபூரணமாக, அவரிடம் ஒப்படைத்தலே, புனித சரணாகதி எனப்படுவதாகும்.

2

“அனுபவிப்பவர்” யார்?

சந்தோஷமும் ஆனந்தமும் நிலையாக, தொடர்ச்சியாக அனுபவித்தல் வேண்டும் என்றே நாம் அனைவரும் ஆசை கொள்கிறோம். நாம் உணர்வுநிலையில்உள்ளவரை,நமதுவிருப்பத்தின் படியோ அல்லது தாமாக நிகழ்வனவற்றையோ, அனுபவித்துக் கொண்டே தான் இருக்கின்றோம். அனுபவத்தை கண்டுகொள்ளும் நாம், “அனுபவிப்பவர்” யார் என்பதை பெரும்பாலும் கண்டுகொள்வதில்லை. ஆழ்ந்த உறக்கம் மற்றும் மயக்கம், ஆகிய தன்னுணர்வு அற்ற நிலையில் ஒருவரால் எந்த அனுபவத்தையும் நுகர இயலாது. உணர்வு நிலையில் ஒருவர் இருக்கும் வரையில் தான், அனுபவித்தல் என்பது சாத்தியமாகும். எனவே, ஒருவரின் உணர்வு நிலைக்கும், நுகர்கின்ற அனுபவத்திற்கும் பெரும் சம்பந்தம் உண்டு. அனுபவத்தின் தன்மை, உணர்வு நிலையின் தன்மையைச் சார்ந்தே அமைகிறது.

இன்பம், துன்பம், பயம் ஆகிய எதுவாயினும், அவைகளை அனுபவிப்பது யார்? நீங்கள் உறங்கும் போது, கனவுகளை அனுபவிப்பது யார்? ஒருவர்

தன்னுடைய இயல்பான உணர்வு நிலையையும், உண்மையான அடையாளத்தையும், உறங்கும் போது மறந்துவிடுவதனால் தான் கனவுகள் எழுகின்றது. தன்னைப் பற்றிய மறதியே கனவுகள் எழ காரணம் ஆகும். உறக்கத்திலிருந்து ஒருவர் சட்டென விழித்து விட்டால், கனவுகள் கொடுத்து வந்த அனுபவங்கள் அந்த கணத்திலேயே நின்றுவிடுகிறது, ஏனெனில் ஒருவர் தனது உண்மையான தன்னுணர்வு நிலையை அடைந்து விடுகிறார். எனவே, “தன்னுணர்வு நிலை” என்பது, அனுபவ நுகர்வுக்கு எதிரானது மட்டும் அல்ல அனுபவங்கள் எழ அனுமதிக்காததும் ஆகும். உங்கள் உறக்கத்தில் கனவுகள் நிகழும் போது, நீங்கள் உறங்கிக் கொண்டிருக்கிறீர்கள் என்பதை மறந்து விடுகிறீர்கள். அந்த கனவில் ஒரு நிகழ்வு அரங்கேறுகிறது. அதில், ஒரு வீதி, வீடுகள், மக்களின் நடமாட்டம், நண்பர்கள், நாய் அல்லது பூனை உலாவிக் கொண்டிருப்பது போன்றவற்றை நீங்கள் பார்க்கிறீர்கள் என வைத்துக் கொள்ளுங்கள், அந்த காட்சியில் நீங்கள் “உங்களை”யும் காண்பீர்கள். அஃதாவது, நீங்கள் உங்கள் உருவத்தையும் அவர்கள் மத்தியில் காண்பீர்கள். அதாவது, ஓர் இடத்தில் நின்று கொண்டு, ஏதோ ஒரு நிறத்தில் உடை அணிந்து கொண்டு, உங்கள் நண்பர்களிடத்தில் உரையாடிக்

கொண்டிருப்பதை காண்பீர்கள். ஒருவேளை, ஒரு நாய் உங்களின் அந்த உருவத்தின் மீது பாய்ந்து கடிக்க முற்பட்டால், நீங்களும் உங்கள் நண்பர்களும் பயந்து, திசைக்கு ஒருவராய் ஓடுகிறீர்கள் என வைத்துக் கொள்ளுங்கள், அப்போது, அந்த தருணத்தில் ஏற்பட்ட பயம் என்ற அனுபவம், உண்மையானது.

நீங்கள் ஓடியது உண்மை. அந்த நாய், வீடுகள், வீதி, அங்கே இருக்கும் மக்கள் மற்றும் அவர்களின் குரல்கள் அனைத்தும் உண்மையே. இப்பொழுது, பயத்தால் பீடிக்கப்பட்டு அந்த முழு நிகழ்வையும்

அனுபவிப்பது யார்? கனவிலே உங்களைப் போன்றே காட்சியளித்த அந்த கனவு உருவத்திற்கு அல்லவா அந்த பயம் என்னும் அனுபவம் ஏற்பட்டது? உண்மையில் “நீங்கள்” என்பது, அந்த கனவு உருவமா, அல்லது படுக்கையில் உறங்கிக் கொண்டிருப்பவரா? நாயைப் பார்த்து பயந்து ஓடிய, உங்களைப் போன்றே காட்சியளித்த அந்த கனவு நபர் அல்லது கனவு உருவம் தான், உண்மையில் “அனுபவித்தவர்.” உண்மையான “நீங்கள்” அல்ல. நீங்கள் அந்த உறக்கத்திலிருந்து விழித்த பின், அந்த நாய், வீதி, வீடுகள், நண்பர்கள், மக்களின் குரல்கள், பயம் ஆகிய அனைத்தும் போலி அல்லது மாயை என்பதை தெளிவாக உணர்கிறீர்கள். இதில் மிக அத்தியாவசியமாக உணர வேண்டியது யாதெனில், “நான்” என கனவில் நிலவி அனுபவித்த அந்த உருவமும் போலி மற்றும் மாயை என்பதே. உங்களின் அனைத்து கனவுகளிலும் இந்த போலி “நான்” என்ற உருவம் தான் அனுபவிப்பவராக திகழ்கின்றதே அன்றி உண்மையான “நான்” அன்று.

இப்போது, உறக்கத்திலிருந்து விழித்த பின், தன்னுணர்வு பெற்ற நிலையில், நனவுலகில், “அனுபவிப்பவர்”என்பவர்யார்?விழித்தபின்,நனவு உலகில் ஏதோ ஒரு பயத்தை அனுபவிக்கிறீர்கள் என வைத்துக் கொள்வோம், அந்த பயத்தினை

உண்மையில் நீங்கள் தான் அனுபவிக்கிறீர்களா அல்லது கனவிலே தோன்றிய அதே கனவு உருவம் அனுபவிக்கிறதா? ஒரு மாயை உருவம் தரித்து உங்கள் கனவிலே தோன்றி உலாவிய அதே போலி “நான்” எனப்படுவது தான், தற்போது நனவிலும் சூட்சுமமாக “அனுபவிப்பவராக” திகழ்கிறது. இந்நிகழ்வை நாம் நனவுலகில் “எண்ணங்கள்” அல்லது “சிந்தனை” என்ற சொற்கூறை பயன்படுத்தி அழைக்கிறோம். ஒருவர், நனவில் பயம் என்ற உணர்வை அனுபவிக்கும் போது, ஒரு காட்சியை மனதில் கற்பனை செய்கிறார். மேலும், அந்த கற்பனையில், கற்பனையான ஓர் இடம், கற்பனையான வேறொரு நபர், பயத்தை தூண்டும் கற்பனையான வஸ்து மற்றும் மிக முக்கியமாக, கற்பனையான “நான்” என்ற உருவத்தை அந்த “எண்ணம்” அல்லது “சிந்தனை” என்கின்ற திரையில் காட்சி படுத்துகிறார். இந்த காட்சியில், கனவில் நிகழ்ந்தது போலவே, “நான்” என்ற அந்த போலி உருவம், அக்காட்சியில் திரையிடப்படும் நிகழ்வுக்கேற்ப பயத்தை அனுபவிக்கத் துவங்குகிறது. ஒரே மாதிரியான நிகழ்வை, உறக்கத்தில்ஏற்படும்போதுகனவுஎன்றும்,நனவில் ஏற்படும் போது சிந்தனை என்றும் அழைத்துக் கொண்டிருக்கிறோம். நாள்தோறும் ஒருவர்க்கு ஏற்படும் சிற்சிறு அனுபவங்கள் கூட இவ்வாறே

ஏற்படுகிறது. ஒருவர் இந்த பேருண்மையை பார்க்க ஆரம்பித்து விட்டால், அதன் பிற்பாடு, அப்பழுக்கற்ற உண்மையான "நான்" எனப்படுவது தனது எல்லையற்ற ஆற்றலால் ஒருவரின் வாழ்வை வழிநடத்த துவங்குகிறது.

நீங்கள் துனபப்படும்போது, உண்மையிலேயே துன்பப்படுகிறீர்களா அல்லது துன்பப்படுவது போல் கற்பனை செய்கிறீர்களா?

துன்பப்படுகையில், கனவைப் போலவே நீங்கள் ஒரு எண்ணத்தை உருவாக்குகிறீர்கள்.

அந்த எண்ண களத்தில், ஏதோ ஒரு குறிப்பிட்ட இடத்தை காண்கிறீர்கள். ஒரு குறிப்பிட்ட மனிதரையும் காண்கிறீர்கள். இவை மட்டும் அல்லாமல் நீங்கள் உங்களையும் அந்த கற்பனை களத்தில், மற்றொருவருடன் உரையாடுவதைப் போல காண்பீர்கள். அந்த காட்சியில், அந்த போலியான "நான்" என்ற உருவம் தனது போலியான முகத்தில், துன்ப பாவனைகளை செய்து கொண்டு துன்பத்தினை அனுபவித்துக் கொண்டிருக்கிறது. உண்மையான "நீங்கள்" அதனை மௌனமாக வேடிக்கை மட்டுமே பார்க்கிறீர்கள். உங்களின் உண்மையான முகம் அதற்கு சமமாக பாவனைகள் செய்வதில்லை. இருப்பினும், அந்த மாயை "நான்," கற்பனையில் அனுபவித்துக் கொண்டிருக்கும் அனுபவத்தின் அதிர்வலைகள் உங்கள் உண்மையான முகத்தில் உடன்நிகழ்வாக வெளிப்படுகிறது. நனவில் எண்ணங்கள் வாயிலாகவும், உறக்கத்தில் கனவு வாயிலாகவும், இந்த கற்பனையான "நான்" தான் அனைத்தையும் அனுபவித்துக் கொண்டிருக்கிறது. உங்களது உண்மையான "நான்" வெறும் சாட்சியாக மட்டுமே உள்ளது. "அனுபவிப்பது" மனமே, விழிப்புணர்வு அல்ல. விழிப்பு நிலையே ஒருவரின் உண்மையான "நான்" எனப்படுவதாகும்.

உங்கள் எண்ணத்தில், உங்கள் நண்பரை காணும்போது, இரண்டு விஷயங்கள் அந்த எண்ணத்துள் நிகழ்கிறது. ஒன்று, உங்கள் கற்பனை நண்பர், மற்றொன்று உங்கள் கற்பனை “நான்.”

அடிப்படையில், நமது திடமான நம்பிக்கை யாதெனில், நமது எண்ணத்தில் எழும் நமது நண்பர் கற்பனைதான், ஆனால் “நான்” நிஜம் என்பது. ஆனால், ஒருவர் தன்னைத் தானே கூர்ந்து கவனித்தால், “நான்” என அனுபவித்துக் கொண்டிருப்பது, ஒரு கற்பனையாகும்.

“அனுபவம்” என்பது ஒரு கற்பனை, “அனுபவிப்பவரும்” ஒரு கற்பனையே.

விழிப்பு நிலையில் தொடர்ச்சியாக மூன்று நிமிடங்களுக்காவது இந்த கற்பனை “நான்” என்ற உருவத்தை சிந்தனையில் எழாதவாரு ஒருவர் பார்த்துக் கொண்டால், அழிவில்லா மௌனத்தை தன்னகத்தே தாங்கி நிற்கும் உண்மையான “நான்” என்பதன் பேரழகை ஒருவர் தரிசிக்கலாகிறார்.

3

முதிர்ச்சியும் ஞானமும்

எந்தெந்த விஷயங்களுக்காக ஒருவர் தனது குழந்தைப் பருவத்தில் துயரங்களை அனுபவித்தாரோ, அதே விஷயங்கள் தற்போது ஏற்பட்டால், அதே துயரத்தினை ஒருவர் தற்போது அடைவது இல்லை. ஒரு பொம்மையை தொலைத்த காரணத்தினாலோ அல்லது ஒரு பொம்மை வேண்டும் என்றோ அல்லது தனது சக நண்பரிடம் ஏற்பட்ட சச்சரவு போன்ற நிகழ்வுகள் அளித்த துயரங்கள், ஒரு குழந்தையானது வளர்ந்து இளைஞனாக ஆன பிறகு, துயரம் அளிப்பது இல்லை. ஒரு பொம்மையுடன் இருந்த உறவைப் பொருத்தவரையில், ஒரு குழந்தையானது அதற்கு ஓர் பெயரிடுகிறது, அலங்காரம் செய்கிறது, அதற்கு உயிர் அளித்து அதனை தனது உடன் பிறந்த ஒன்றாகவோ அல்லது நண்பனாகவோ பாவித்து அந்த பொம்மையை பாதுகாக்கிறது.

அதன் மீது பெறும் பற்று கொண்டு அப்பற்றின் விளைவாக ஏற்படும் இன்பத்தையோ அல்லது துன்பத்தையோ அனுபவிக்கின்றது. அதே குழந்தை, வளர்ச்சி அடைந்து ஓர் இளைஞனாக ஆன பிறகு, அந்த பொம்மையின் மேல் வைத்திருந்த பற்றினையும் உணர்வினையும் தாமாக நீக்கிக் கொள்கிறது. இதன் விளைவாக அந்த பொம்மை சம்பந்தப்பட்ட விஷயங்களிலிருந்து, இன்பம் அல்லது துன்பம் போன்ற அனுபவங்கள் ஏற்படுவது இல்லை. அதே போன்று, இளமை பருவத்தில் ஏற்பட்ட பிரச்சனைகளும் துயரங்களும், நடுத்தர வயது அடைந்தவுடன் தாமாக நீங்கிவிடுகிறது. ஒரு முதியவர் தனது குழந்தை பருவ, இளமை பருவ, நடுத்தர பருவ பிரச்சனைகளையும் துயரங்களையும் கடந்து

விட்டமையால், அவர் அப் பிரச்சனைகளுக்கும் துயரங்களுக்கும் சரியான முறையில் தீர்வுகளை கண்டுபிடித்த பின் அவைகளை கடந்தார் என்று பொருளில்லை. ஒரு பருவத்திலிருந்து இன்னொரு பருவத்திற்கு மாறும் போது, முந்தைய பருவத்தின் பிரச்சனைகளும் துயரங்களும் தாமாகவே மறைந்து விடுகிறது. ஒவ்வொரு பருவத்திலும் அனுபவித்த பிரச்சனைகளுக்கும் துயரங்களுக்கும் தீர்வை அளித்தது, ஒருவரின் கரைகண்ட அனுபவமோ அல்லது பரந்த அறிவோ அல்ல! விழிப்புணர்வில் தாமாக ஏற்பட்ட மாற்றும் அல்லது வளர்ச்சி தான் காரணம். ஒரு பருவத்தின் அனுபவங்களை அதே தளத்தில் இயங்கும் விழிப்புணர்வு நிலையால் வெற்றி கொள்ள இயலாது. ஏனெனில், ஒரு பருவத்தில் இயங்கும் மனோபாவம், அதே தளத்தில் உள்ள விழிப்புணர்வு நிலை ஏற்படுத்திய உருவாக்கமே. ஒரு குறிப்பிட்ட விழிப்புணர்வு நிலையே, ஒரு குறிப்பிட்ட மனோபாவத்தை வெளிப்படுத்துகிறது. மனோபாவம் எவ்வகையோ, பெறும் அனுபவங்களும் அவ்வகையே. உறக்கத்தின் போது பதற்றமூட்டும் கனவைக் கண்டு ஒருவர் ஏன் அஞ்சுகிறார் என்றால், ஒருவரின் விழிப்புணர்வு நிலை, அதே கனவு நிலையில் அதே தளத்தில் வாசம் செய்வதால் தான். அதே தளத்தில் இயங்கும் விழிப்புணர்வால் அவ்வச்சத்தை

வேரோடு சாய்த்தல் என்பது இயலாத காரியம். தூக்கத்திலிருந்து விழிப்பதே, அவ்வச்சத்தை வேரோடு ஒழிப்பது ஆகும். ஒரு நிலையில் இருந்து அடுத்த மேல் நிலைக்கு விழிப்புணர்வு வளர்ச்சி அடைவதே, முந்தைய கீழ் நிலையின் மொத்த பிரச்சனைகளுக்கும் அனுபவங்களுக்கும் தீர்வு பயக்கும். குழந்தை பருவத்தில் இருந்து இளமை பருவத்திற்கும், இளமை பருவத்தில் இருந்து முதுமை பருவத்திற்கும் வளர்ச்சி அடையும் விழிப்புணர்வு நிலைக்கு "முதிர்ச்சி" எனப் பெயர். நிலவு எவ்வாறு அமாவாசை முதல் பௌர்ணமி வரை ஒவ்வொரு கட்டமாக வளர்ந்து முழுமை பெறுகிறதோ, அவ்வாறே நமது மனமும் ஒவ்வொரு கட்டமாக வளர்ந்து முதிர்ச்சி அடைகிறது. நிலவு எவ்வாறு சூரியனிடமிருந்து ஒளியைப் பெற்று பூமிக்கு வழங்குகிறதோ அல்லது சூரியன் எவ்வாறு நிலவை ஒரு ஊடகமாக பயன்படுத்தி இரவில் பூமிக்கு ஒளியை நல்குகிறதோ, அவ்வாறே, சூரியனாக விளங்கும் "நான்" என்ற தன்னுணர்வு, மனம் என்ற நிலவுக்கு விழிப்புணர்வு என்ற ஒளியை பாய்ச்சுகிறது. நிலவின் ஊடாக வரும் சூரிய ஒளி எவ்வாறு உஷ்ணம் தணிந்து முற்றிலும் வேறோர் ஒளியாக உணரப்படுகிறதோ, அவ்வாறே, மனதின் வழியாக வெளிப்படும் விழிப்புணர்வு, உண்மையான "நான்" என்பதன் முழுமையான

விழிப்புணர்வு நிலையில் இருந்து முற்றிலும் மாறுபட்டது. மனதின் விழிப்புணர்வு நிலை சோர்வு, உபாதை, அதிர்ச்சி, பயம், ஆச்சரியம், ஆனந்தம் போன்ற பல்வேறு சமயங்களில் விரிந்து மற்றும் சுருங்கும் தன்மையுடையது. உறக்கத்திலும் மயக்கத்திலும் அற்று இருப்பது. அது உடலுக்கும் அதன் இரசாயன மற்றும் வேதியியலுக்கும் கட்டுப்பட்டது. ஆனால், "நான்" என்ற தன்னுணர்வின் விழிப்பு நிலை, சூரியனைப் போன்று அனைத்து சமயங்களிலும் எந்தவித மாற்றமும் இல்லாமல் ஒரே போன்று, நிலைத்து நின்ற வண்ணமே இருக்கக்கூடியது. ஆழ்ந்த உறக்கத்திலும் கூட "நான்" என்பது தன்னுணர்வுடனேயே தொடரக்கூடியது. வளர்பிறையாய் ஒவ்வொரு கட்டமாக வளர்ந்து ஒளியை அதிகரித்துக் கொள்ளும் நிலவு போல, ஒவ்வொரு பருவத்திலும் மனதிலே வளர்ச்சி பெறும் விழிப்புணர்வு நிலையை "முதிர்ச்சி" என நாம் அழைக்கிறோம். வெகுகாலமாக மனதில் மட்டுமே வாசம் செய்து, மனோபாவத்தில் மட்டும் முதிர்ச்சி என்ற நிலையை அடைந்து வந்த நாம், நமது கவனத்தை, மனதிற்கு விழிப்புணர்வை பாய்ச்சும் "நான்" என்ற தன்னுணர்வு மேல் வைத்தால், அது "ஞானம்" என்று அழைக்கப்படுகிறது. அனைத்து மனோபாவ சிறையில் இருந்தும் ஒருவரை ஞானம்

மட்டுமே மீட்டெடுக்கிறது. மனோபாவத்தின் வீழ்ச்சி, துயரங்களின் வீழ்ச்சியாகும். ஆழ்ந்த உறக்கமும், மரணமும் தொட முடியாத இந்த ஞானத்தை பெற, ஒருவர் தன் முக பாவனைகள் மற்றும் உடல் அசைவுகளை தொடர்ச்சியாக வெறுமனே கவனித்து வந்தால், இது நாள் வரை மனதில் மட்டுமே வாசம் செய்து வந்த ஒருவரது கவனம், “நான்” என்ற தன்னுணர்வு உடன் வாசம் செய்து ஞானத்திற்கு வழிவகுக்கிறது.

4

எண்ண சக்கரத்தின் அச்சாணி

மனோதத்துவ நிபுணர்களின் கூற்றுப்படி, ஒரு குழந்தையானது எப்பொழுதும் "தேவை" என்ற நிலைப்பாட்டில் உள்ளது. அது எப்பொழுதும் "பெற்றுக் கொள்கின்ற" இடத்தில் உள்ளது. அது "கொடுக்கும்" இடத்தில் இல்லை. அதற்கு உணவு, அன்பு, அக்கறை, பாதுகாப்பு, கவனம், புகழ்ச்சி போன்றவை தேவைப்படுகிறது. இவை அனைத்தையும் ஒரு குழந்தை, தன் பெற்றோர்களிடத்தில் மட்டுமின்றி தன்னைச் சுற்றி உள்ள தனது உறவினர்கள், அக்கம் பக்கத்தினர் அனைவரிடத்திலும் பெறுகிறது. அந்த குழந்தையை எங்கு கொண்டு சென்றாலும், அது சுற்றிவளைக்கப்பட்டு அன்பு, கவனம், அக்கறை மற்றும் புகழ்ச்சியானது மற்றவர்களால் வழங்கப்படுகிறது.

அக்குழந்தை "தானே" அனைவருடைய கவனத்தின் மையம் என உணர ஆரம்பிக்கிறது. தன்னைச் சுற்றியுள்ள உலகமே தன்னை பேணுகிறது, அக்கறை செலுத்துகிறது, புகழ்ந்து பேசுகிறது என்றும், தன்னைப் பற்றியே அனைவரும் சிந்தித்துக் கொண்டிருக்கின்றனர் என்றும் தன்னுள் நம்ப ஆரம்பிக்கிறது. அனைவரின் கவனத்தின் மையமாக இருப்பதில் ஒரு முழுமையான பாதுகாப்பை அக்குழந்தை உணர்கிறது. தான் அனைவரின் கவனத்தின் மையம் என்ற இந்த நம்பிக்கையானது அக்குழந்தையின் மெல்லிய மனதில் ஆழமாக பதிந்து விடுகிறது. பிறரின் கவனம், அன்பு, அக்கறையை பெற சில

சமயங்களில், தான் வேதனையில் இருப்பதாக பாசாங்கு செய்கிறது. வேதனையில் வாடுவது பிறரின் கவனத்தை தன்பால் அதிகமாக ஈர்ப்பதால், ஒரு குழந்தை, தன்னை அறியாமலேயே சுயபரிதாப மனப்பான்மையை வளர்த்துக் கொள்கிறது. இதன் காரணமாக அதன் மனம், துன்பத்திற்கும் துயரத்திற்கும் அதிக மதிப்பீடு மற்றும் முக்கியத்துவத்தை அளித்துவிடுகிறது. இதன் பின்னர், ஒரு குழந்தையின் ஒட்டுமொத்த மனதின் கட்டமைப்பும் "தானே அனைவர் கவனத்தின் மையம்" என்று நிலைகொள்கிறது. அன்பு, கவனம், புகழ்ச்சி ஆகியவைகளால், பாதுகாப்பு மற்றும் மகிழ்ச்சி நிரம்பிய அனுபவங்களைப் பெற்ற அந்த மனம், வளர வளர, அதே அனுபவத்தை மீண்டும் மீண்டும் நுகர முயல்கிறது. மனதினுடைய இந்த குறிப்பிட்ட ஆசையே, மனிதனுடைய பல்வேறு ஆசைகளுக்கு அடித்தளமாக அமைந்திருக்கிறது. இந்த குழந்தைப் பருவ மனப்பாங்கின் தூண்டுதலின் அடிப்படையிலேயே ஒருவரது சிந்தனை அமைகிறது, செயல்கள் மேற்கொள்ளப்படுகிறது மற்றும் குறிக்கோள்கள் நிர்ணயம் செய்யப்படுகிறது. முதிர்ந்த மனிதர்கள் கூட தன்னை அறியாமலேயே இந்த குழந்தை தனத்தை, சிறுபிள்ளை தனத்தை பற்றிக் கொண்டு வாழ்நாள் முழுவதும், அடுத்தவரின் கவனத்தை

தன்பால் ஈர்க்கும் முயற்சியிலேயே தனது முழு வாழ்வையும் கழிக்கின்றனர். இப்படியாக, ஒவ்வொரு மனிதரும், “உலகமே தனை சூழ்ந்து புகழ வேண்டும், கைதட்டி அங்கீகரிக்க வேண்டும், கவனம் செலுத்த வேண்டும்” என்ற மனதிட்பம் கொண்டுள்ளனர். உலகத்தையே அவ்வாறு தன்பால் ஈர்க்க முடியாவிட்டாலும், ஒரு நகர மக்களின் கவனத்தையாவது ஈர்க்க வேண்டும், அதுவும் முடியாவிட்டால் குறைந்தபட்சம் குறிப்பிட்ட சிலறின் கவனத்தையும் புகழ்ச்சியையுமாவது பெற வேண்டும் என்ற ஒற்றை நோக்கத்துடனேயே சிந்தனைகள் அமைக்கப்பட்டு, செயல்கள் மேற்கொள்ளப்படுகிறது. இந்த குழந்தை மனப்பான்மை, “வேண்டும்” அல்லது “பெருகின்ற முனை”யில் தன்னை பலமாக நிலைநிறுத்திக் கொண்டுள்ளது. உடல் வளர்ந்து முதுமையை அடைந்தாலும், இந்த குழந்தை மனப்பான்மையே, வாழ்நாள் முழுக்க உயிர்ப்புடன் வினை ஆற்றுகிறது. மனதை, இந்த குழந்தைத் தன மனோபாவம் சிறைபிடித்து வைத்திருப்பதை பெரும்பாலும் ஒருவர் உணர்வதில்லை. முதுமை மற்றும் அதிக அனுபவங்கள் பெற்ற காரணத்தினால், ஒருவர், “முதிர்ச்சி” என ஒன்றை அடையாளப் படுத்திக் கொள்வது, விளையாடிக் கொண்டிருந்த பொம்மைகளை மாற்றிக் கொண்டமையாலே

அன்றி, விளையாட்டை மாற்றிக் கொண்டதால் அல்ல. குழந்தைப் பருவம் முதல் முதுமைப் பருவம் வரை அதே விளையாட்டு, அதே விதிமுறைகளோடு, அதே எதிர்ப்பார்ப்புடனேயே ஒருவரால் விளையாடப் படுகிறது. ஒவ்வொரு வயதிற்கு ஏற்ப பொம்மைகள் மட்டுமே மாறுகிறது.

மனதின் துன்பங்கள், துயரங்கள், வலி, பொறாமை, வெறுப்புணர்ச்சி, வன்முறை, பாவச் செயல்கள் அனைத்தும் பெரும்பாலும் இந்த மன நிலைப்பாட்டின் விளைவே ஆகும். ஒருவர் தன்னுடைய எண்ண ஓட்டங்களை கவனித்தால், ஒவ்வொரு எண்ணத்தின் அடி நாதமும் "தற்பெருமையாகவே" இருக்கும். ஒருவர் சிந்திக்கையில், அடுத்தவர் தன் வாதத்தை ஏற்றுக் கொள்பதாகவும், தன்னை புகழும்படியாகவுமே சிந்திக்கிறார். "வேண்டும்" அல்லது "பெறுகின்ற முனை"யில் பலமாக நிலைப் பெற்றிருக்கும் மனம், அன்பையும் கவனத்தையும் அடுத்தவருக்கு "கொடுக்கும்" சூழலில் இருந்தாலும், அடுத்தவர் அதே அன்பையும் கவனத்தையும் திரும்ப தனக்கு அளிக்கிறார்களா என "பெறுகின்ற முனை"யில் இருந்துகொண்டு தான் "கொடுக்கும்" செயலை புரியும். அன்பையும் கவனத்தையும் "பெறும்" முனைப்புடனேயே, அன்பையும் கவனத்தையும் பிறருக்கு "கொடுக்கும்." எண்ணங்கள் எனும்

ஓயாமல் சுற்றிக் கொண்டிருக்கும் சக்கரத்திலிருந்து, தற்பெருமை எனும் அச்சாணியை ஒருவர் நீக்கிவிட்டால், எப்பொழுதும் கற்பனைகளால் நிரம்பி வழியும் "வேண்டும்" என்ற குழந்தை மனோபாவம் ஏற்படுத்திய சிறையில் இருந்து ஒருவர் தன்னை விடுவித்துக் கொள்கிறார். அத்துடன், இதுநாள்வரை "கவனம் வேண்டும்" என்ற மனநிலையின் காரணத்தினால் அனுபவித்து வந்த மன அழுத்தம், விரக்தி, ஏமாற்றம் ஆகியவைகளில் இருந்தும் விடுதலை பெறுகிறார். விடுதலைப் பெற்ற அந்த மனம், முதன்முறையாக பரிபூரணமாக "கொடுக்கும் முனை"க்கு மாறுகிறது. வாழ்நாள் முழுவதும் பலனை நோக்கியே வினையாற்றிய ஒரு மனிதர், முதன்முறையாக பலனை எதிர்பாராமல், ஆற்றப்படும் செயலுக்கே முக்கியத்துவம் அளிக்கிறார். அடுத்தவருக்கு தான் வழங்கும் அன்பு, நிபந்தனைகள் இன்றி, வழங்கும் அழகிற்காக மட்டுமே வழங்கப்படுகிறது.

ஒருவர் ஆனந்தமாக இருக்கும் போது "கொடுக்கும் முனை"யில் உள்ளார். உண்மையான அன்பு என்பது ஆனந்தத்தின் வெளிப்பாடாகும். பொதுவாக, ஆனந்தம் என்பது அன்பின் வெளிப்பாடு என நாம் நம்புகிறோம். ஆனால் உண்மை நேர்மாறானது. ஆனந்தமாக இருக்கும் ஒருவரால் தான் அன்பு செலுத்தவே இயலும்.

உண்மையான அன்பு வெளிப்பட, ஆனந்தம் தேவைப்படுகிறது. ஆனந்தத்தை அடைய, மன அமைதி தேவைப்படுகிறது. மனம் அமைதி பெற, கற்பனையின் நிறுத்தம் தேவைப்படுகிறது. கற்பனைகள் நிற்க, தற்புகழ்ச்சியின்மை தேவைப்படுகிறது. எனவே, தற்புகழ்ச்சியின் அளவே, ஒருவருடைய அமைதியின் அளவு, ஆனந்தத்தின் அளவு மற்றும் அன்பின் அளவை தீர்மானிக்கின்றது. எண்ணங்களில் தற்புகழ்ச்சி நிலவினாலும், ஒருவரால் தூய அன்பு செலுத்த இயலும். இருப்பினும், அவ்வகை எண்ணங்களை அகற்றி அமைதி பெற்ற மனம், “வேதனை” என்ற சிறையில் இருந்து விடுபட்டு, பாரபட்சமில்லாத மற்றும் எதையும் எதிர்பார்க்காத அன்பை மட்டுமே வெளிப்படுத்துகிறது.

ஒருவருள் இருக்கும் அன்பின் அளவே, அவரின் சிந்திக்கும் விதம், நோக்கம், எடுக்கும் முடிவுகள் மற்றும் வாழ்வைப் பற்றிய கண்ணோட்டத்தை தீர்மானிக்கிறது. சிந்திக்கும் விதம், நோக்கம், எடுக்கும் முடிவுகள், கண்ணோட்டம் ஆகியவையே உண்மையில் “அறிவு” எனப்படுவதாகும். ஆகவே, ஒருவர் பெற்றிருக்கும் அன்பின் அளவே அவர் பெற்றிருக்கும் அறிவின் அளவும் ஆகும்.

5

மனமும் அதன் கட்டுப்பாடும்

அடையாளப்படுத்திக் கொள்ளுதல் :

தொலைக்காட்சியில் ஒரு சினிமா படம் பார்க்கையில், அதில் வரும் ஏதோ ஒரு கதாபாத்திரத்துடன் தன்னை அடையாளப் படுத்திக் கொண்டு, ஒருவர் போலியான அனுபவத்தை அனுபவிக்க துவங்குகிறார்.

தொலைக்காட்சி பெட்டி சற்று தொலைவில் இருப்பதால், தன்னிடமிருந்து அது வேறானது

என ஒருவரால் உணர்ந்து கொள்ள முடிகிறது. தொலைக்காட்சி பெட்டியைப் போன்றே, நமது மனமும் ஒரு காணொளியை, நம் விழிப்புணர்வுக்கு மிக அருகாமையில் ஒளிபரப்புகிறது. நாம், நமது மனம் ஒவ்வொரு முறையம் ஒளிபரப்பும் ஏதோ ஒரு காணொளியுடன் நம்மை முழுவதுமாக அடையாளப் படுத்திக் கொண்டு, அதனை அனுபவிக்கலாகிறோம். காற்று வாசனையாக மாறுவதைப் போல, எண்ணங்களோடு அடையாளப் படுத்திக் கொள்ளும் விழிப்புணர்வு, எண்ணங்களாகவே மாறிவிடுகிறது.

“ஒருவர் என்ன நினைக்கிறாரோ, அதுவாகவே மாறுகிறார்” என்ற கூற்று நெடுங்காலமாகவே மிகத் தவறாக புரிந்து கொள்ளப்பட்டு, சமுதாயத்தில் பரப்பப்பட்டும் வருகிறது. அஃதாவது, வாழ்வில் எதையாவது அடைய விரும்புவோர், அதனைப் பற்றியே எப்பொழுதும் எண்ணிக் கொண்டிருந்தால், அந்த எண்ணத்தின் சக்தியானது அவர் விரும்பியவற்றை விரும்பியவாறே நிகழ்த்திக் காட்டும் என்ற சித்தாந்தம், நெடுங்காலமாய் மக்களின் மத்தியில் நிலவிக் கொண்டிருக்கிறது. இந்த சித்தாந்தத்தை சற்றே ஆராய்ந்தீர்கள் என்றால், இதில் எந்த அடிப்படை உண்மையும் இல்லை என்பது விளங்கும். மனிதன், தன்னை திருப்தி படுத்திக்கொள்ள படைத்த இத்தகைய

குறுகிய சித்தாந்தத்திற்குள், இந்த மாபெரும் வாழ்வானது வளைந்து நுழையாது. "நீங்கள் என்ன எண்ணுகிறீர்களோ, அதுவாகவே மாறுகிறீர்கள்" என்ற கூற்று முற்றிலும் வேறொரு பரிமாணத்தைக் கொண்டது. அதாவது, ஒருவருக்கு எண்ணங்கள் நிகழ்ந்து கொண்டிருக்கும் அந்த தருவாயில், ஒருவர் நிகழ்ந்து கொண்டிருக்கும் அந்த எண்ணங்களாகவே மாறுகிறார் என்பதே அதன் உண்மை பொருள். உறங்கும் போது கனவுகள் ஏற்படுகிறது. நாம் படுக்கையில் உறங்கிக் கொண்டு இருக்கிறோம் என்ற உண்மையை மறந்து, அந்த கனவே உண்மை என அதனுடன் நம்மை முழுவதுமாக அடையாளப் படுத்திக் கொண்டு, அந்த கனவாகவே நாம் மாறி அந்த கனவுலகில் வாழ்வதைப் போல, எண்ணங்கள் எழும்போது அதனுடன் நம்மை அடையாளப் படுத்திக் கொண்டு அந்த எண்ணங்களாகவே நாம் மாறுகிறோம். துன்ப எண்ணங்கள் எழும் போது, நாம் துன்பமாக மாறுகிறோம்; இன்ப எண்ணங்கள் எழும் போது, நாம் இன்பமாக மாறுகிறோம்; பய எண்ணங்கள் எழும் போது, நாம் பயமாக மாறுகிறோம். நீங்கள் என்ன எண்ணுகிறீர்களோ அதுவாகவே மாறுகிறீர்கள்.

"அடையாளப் படுத்திக் கொள்ளுதல்" என்பது மனதின் மேலோங்கிய மற்றும் ஆளுமைமிக்க பண்புக்கூறு ஆகும். மனம் எப்பொழுதும் அதனை

ஏதோ ஒரு காட்சியுடன் அடையாளப் படுத்திக் கொண்டு, அடையாளப் படுத்திக் கொண்ட அந்த காட்சியிலிருந்து இன்பத்தையோ அல்லது துன்பத்தையோ அனுபவித்துக் கொண்டு தான் இருக்கும். மனதின் இந்த அடையாளப் படுத்திக் கொள்ளும் பண்புக்கூறு மிக ஆளுமைமிக்கது என்பதாலும், அதனை தடுப்பது மிகக் கடினம் என்ற காரணத்தினாலும், “பேருண்மையுடன்” அடையாளப் படுத்திக் கொள்ள பரிந்துரை செய்யப் படுகிறது. மகா மௌனம் பொருந்திய தனது விழிப்புணர்வுடன் மனம் தன்னை அடையாளப் படுத்திக் கொள்ளும் போது, அந்த மகா மௌனமாகவே மனமானது மாறுகிறது.

புராணக் கதைகளும், ஆழ்மனமும் :

பழங்கால புராணக் கதைகள், சான்றோர்களால், அறம், நன்னடத்தை, வினைப் பயன் இவைகளின் முக்கியத்துவத்தை மையமாகக் கொண்டு வளமான இலக்கிய நயத்துடன் எழுதப்பட்டிருந்த போதிலும், எதற்காக அக்கதைகளில் முற்றிலும் முரணான, நிஜ உலகில் சாத்தியமற்ற, பகுத்தறிவை மீறிய பல சம்பவங்கள் குறிப்பிடப் படுகிறது என்ற வினாவும் எண்ணமும் ஒவ்வொருவர் மனதிலும் எழத்தான் செய்கிறது. ஒரு சிலர் இதற்கு எதிர்வினை ஆற்றுபவராகவும், வேறு சிலர்

மரபுசார்ந்த நம்பிக்கையுடன் அவற்றை அப்படியே ஏற்றுக்கொள்பவராகவும் உள்ளனர்.

உறங்கும்போது ஒருவர்க்கு ஏற்படும் கனவுகளை கவனித்துப் பார்த்தால், அந்த கனவுகளில் முற்றிலும் முரணான, நிஜ உலகில் சாத்தியமற்ற, பகுத்தறிவை மீறிய சம்பவங்கள் நடைபெறுவதை காண முடியும். ஏற்கனவே இறந்துவிட்ட ஒரு நபர் கனவில் தோன்றும் போது, அவர் இறந்துவிட்டவர் என்ற முழு தன்னுணர்வுடனேயே நாம் அவரிடத்தில் உரையாடிக் கொண்டிருப்போம். இது போன்று சாத்தியமற்ற, பகுத்தறிவுக்கு மீறிய பல சம்பவங்களை தினந்தோறும் நாம் கனவில் கண்டுகொண்டு தான் இருக்கிறோம். இவை அனைத்தும் சாத்தியமற்றது மற்றும் பகுத்தறிவை மீறியது என, கனவு காண்கின்ற அந்த தருணத்தில் பகுத்தறிவுவாதிகள் உட்பட யாருமே உணர்வதில்லை. நனவுலகை கண்ட அதே மனிதர் தான் கனவையும் காண்கிறார். பின் எதற்காக ஒரே மனிதர், கனவின் சாத்தியமற்ற, பகுத்தறிவை மீறிய சம்பவங்களை, உண்மையென அப்படியே ஏற்றுக் கொள்கிறார்? நாம், பகுத்தறிவு பொருந்திய மேல் மனதை மட்டுமே சார்ந்த ஜீவன்கள் அல்ல. மனதின் அனைத்து உட்கூறுகளையும் சார்ந்தவர்கள் ஆவோம். மேல்

மனதை விட ஆழ்மனம் மிகவும் சக்தி வாய்ந்தது. மேல் மனதின் சீரான இயக்கத்திற்கு, ஆழ்மனதின் சீரான இயக்கம் அவசியமாகிறது. ஆழ்மனதின் ஒரு பகுதி, அதிசய நிகழ்வுகளிலும், சாத்தியமற்ற நிகழ்வுகளிலும் தன்னை திருப்திபடுத்திக் கொள்கிறது. பகுத்தறிவிற்கு உட்பட்ட மேல் மனதுக்கும், பகுத்தறிவை மீறிய ஆழ்மனதுக்கும் இடையே சமச்சீர் போக்கை ஏற்படுத்தி, மனதின் இந்த இரண்டு பண்புகூறுகளுக்கும் உரிய நியாயம் செய்ய, சான்றோர்களால் சான்றான்மையுடன் எழுதப்பட்டவையே புராணக் கதைகள் ஆகும்.

நனவுலகில், நாம் வெறும் மேல் மனதுடன் மட்டும் வாழ்வதில்லை. ஆழ்மன செயற்பாட்டுடன், முழு மனதுடன் தான் எப்போதும் வாழ்ந்து கொண்டு இருக்கிறோம். மேலும், ஆழ்மனம் எதற்காக சாத்தியமற்ற சம்பவங்களை தோற்றுவிக்கிறது? ஆழ்மனம் என்றழைக்கப்படும் உள் மனதிற்கு, இயல்பாகவே இயற்கை விதிகளை மீறிய அதிசய நிகழ்வுகளின் மீது நாட்டம் உண்டு. ஏனெனில், ஆழ்மனதிற்கு இயற்கை விதிகளை மீறி செயல்படும் சக்தியும் ஆற்றலும் இயல்பாகவே உண்டு. விஞ்ஞான கண்டுபிடிப்புகள் அனைத்தும், ஆழ்மனம் விஞ்ஞானிகளுக்கு அளித்த கொடையே ஆகும். ஒரு விஞ்ஞானி, அவரின் ஆராய்ச்சியைப் பற்றி தன்னால் இயன்றவரை சிந்தித்து விட்ட பிறகு,

ஆழ்மனம், அந்த ஆய்வைப் பற்றிய உண்மையை, அவருக்கு கொடையாக வழங்குகிறது. மனதின் ஒரு பகுதி மட்டுமே, இந்த தொட்டு உணரும் இயற்பியல் உலகத்தோடு தொடர்புடையது. அதனின் வேர், இந்த இயற்பியல் உலகத்தை சார்ந்தது இல்லை.

எண்ணங்களின் கட்டுப்பாடு :

நேர்மறை எண்ணங்களோ அல்லது எதிர்மறை எண்ணங்களோ எதுவாயினும், அவை உள் அமைதியை குலைக்கும் சாதனமாகும். அனைத்து அனுபவங்களுக்கும் மனமே காரணம் என்பதால், லௌகீக வாழ்வு சிறக்க அதன் கட்டுப்பாடும், ஆன்மீக அறிதலுக்கு மனதின் அசைவின்மையும் தேவைப்படுகிறது.

மனதில் எழும் ஒரு எண்ணத்தை இரண்டு நிமிடங்கள் ஒருவர் தாமதப்படுத்தி, பிறகு சிந்திக்கத் துவங்கினால், மனம் கட்டுக்குள் வருகிறது. மனதில் ஒரு எண்ணம் எழும்போது, அதனை பத்து விநாடிகளுக்கு காலங்கடத்தி, பிறகு அந்த சிந்தனையை மேற்கொள்ள வேண்டும். இப்பயிற்சியை ஒரு குறிப்பிட்ட நேரம் ஒதுக்கி செய்வதைக் காட்டிலும், மனதில் நிகழ்ந்து கொண்டிருக்கும் ஒரு எண்ணத்தை சட்டென பத்து விநாடிகளுக்கு நிறுத்தி, அதன் பின் அதே எண்ண

ஓட்டத்தை அனுமதிப்பது சாலச் சிறந்தது. இதே போன்று, மெல்ல மெல்ல பத்து விநாடிகளில் இருந்து குறைந்த பட்சம் இரண்டு நிமிடங்களுக்கும் மேலாக நீட்டிக்க வேண்டும். இவ்வாறு செவ்வனே செய்யும்போது, எண்ணங்கள் உங்களை கட்டுப்படுத்துவது மாறி நீங்கள் எண்ணங்களை கட்டுப்படுத்த துவங்குகிறீர்கள். ஒரு எண்ணத்தில், அறிவு, மிதமிஞ்சிய கற்பனை, பயம், சோகம் போன்ற அழுத்தமான உணர்வுகள் கலவையாக உள்ளன. ஓர் எண்ணம் எழும் கணத்தில் அதை நிறுத்தி, சில நிமிடங்கள் கழித்து வேறோர் கணத்தில் அதை அனுமதிக்கும் போது, அந்த எண்ணத்தின் "அறிவு" பகுதி மட்டும் மிஞ்சி, எதிர்மறை பகுதிகளின் வீரியம் குறைக்கப் படுகிறது. எண்ணங்களில் எதிர்மறை பண்புகளான பயம், சோகம், விரக்தி போன்றவற்றின் வீரியம் குறையும் போது, மனதில், எண்ணங்களின் வேகம் குறைந்து, மெதுவாகவும் சாந்தமாகவும் நகர்கிறது. அதுமட்டுமின்றி, உறங்கும்போது தோன்றும் கனவுகளிலும் நேர்மறை மாற்றம் நிகழ்கிறது. ஒரு துன்ப எண்ணத்தையோ அல்லது பய எண்ணத்தையோ இரண்டு நிமிடங்கள் தாமதப்படுத்தி பின் அனுமதிக்கும் போது, இரண்டு நிமிடங்களுக்கு முன்பு இருந்த அதே வீரியத்துடன் துன்பமும் பயமும் இருப்பதில்லை. மீண்டும்

தொடர்ந்து இன்னொரு இரண்டு நிமிடங்கள் அதனை சிந்திக்காமல் தாமதப்படுத்தும் போது, அந்த எண்ணங்கள் மனதில் முன்பு போல் எழாமல் வலுவிழந்து விடும். இவ்வகை பயிற்சியை ஆரம்ப கட்டத்தில், நம்முள் எழும் ஓர் சாதாரண எண்ணத்தை தாமதப்படுத்தி பயில வேண்டும். அப்பொழுது தான் மும்முரமாக எழும் பய மற்றும் துன்ப எண்ணங்களை சிரமம் இல்லாமல் தாமதப்படுத்த இயலும்.

மனதின் அசைவின்மை :

ஆழ்ந்த உறக்கம் மற்றும் மயக்கம், இவற்றைத் தவிர்த்து, மனமானது தொடர்ந்து செயல்பட்டுக் கொண்டே இருக்கிறது. ஆழ்ந்த உறக்கத்தின் விவரிக்கமுடியாதஆனந்தத்தையேஒருவர்பெரிதும் விரும்புகிறார்,ஏனெனில்,அங்கே"அனுபவிப்பவர்" முற்றிலுமாக இல்லை. எண்ணங்கள் எழாமல் இருக்கும் போது, "அனுபவிப்பவரும்" எழாமல் இருக்கிறார். "அனுபவிப்பவர்" இல்லாத அந்த நிலையுடன் நனவில் விழிப்புணர்வோடு இருந்து, ஆழ்ந்த உறக்கத்தின் ஆனந்த நிலையை நனவிலே அடைவதற்கு, சமாதிநிலை எனப் பெயர்.

. ஆழ்ந்த உறக்கத்திற்கு, "நான்" என்ற உணர்வும், எண்ணங்களும் தடையாக விளங்கிய போது, மனமுவந்து அதனை துறக்க எவ்வாறு

ஒருவர் சித்தமானாரோ, அது போலவே, சரியான முயற்சி மேற்கொண்டு, நனவில் விழிப்புடன் எண்ணங்களை துறந்து, மன அசைவின்மையை அடைந்தால், மறை நூல்கள் சுட்டிக் காட்டிய மறைபொருள் விளங்குகிறது.

மனதின் அசைவின்மைக்கு, எண்ணங்களின் ஆணிவேரை அறிந்து அதனை துண்டித்தல் வேண்டும். ஒரு மனிதராக நாம், எப்பொழுதும் அடுத்த மனிதர்களிடத்தில் உறவு பேணுகிறோம். நமது எண்ணங்களை ஆட்கொண்டு இருப்பது இந்த "அடுத்தவரே" ஆவர். இந்த "அடுத்தவரே" நமது எண்ணங்கள் முழுவதையும் வியாபித்து இருப்பது. "அடுத்தவரே" சிந்தனையின் மிக முக்கிய அம்சம். நமது எண்ணங்களில் "அடுத்தவர்" இல்லை என்றால் சிந்தனையே நடைபெறாது. எனவே, "அடுத்தவர்" என்பதே எண்ணங்களின் ஆணிவேர் ஆகும். எண்ணங்களில் மூன்று கூறுகள் சம்பந்தப்பட்டுள்ளன. அவை "நான்," "அடுத்தவர்," மற்றும் "பேச்சு." இந்த மூன்றில், ஏதேனும் ஒன்றை ஒருவர் நிறுத்தினால், மற்ற இரண்டும் தாமாகவே விலகிவிடும். "நான்" என்ற எண்ணத்தை, அஃதாவது, சிந்தனையில், தன்னைத் தானே ஒரு உடையில், ஏதோ ஒரு இடத்தில், நின்றுகொண்டோ அல்லது அமர்ந்துகொண்டோ இருப்பதைப் போன்று கற்பனை செய்யாமல் பார்த்துக் கொண்டால், மற்ற

இரண்டு கூறுகளான "அடுத்தவர்" மற்றும் "பேச்சு" தாமாக எண்ணங்களில் இருந்து விலகி விடுகிறது. அல்லது, "அடுத்தவர்" (உங்கள் உறவினரோ அல்லது நண்பரோ) உங்கள் எண்ணங்களில் வராமல் பார்த்துக் கொண்டால், மற்ற இரண்டு கூறுகளான "நான்" மற்றும் "பேச்சு," தாமாக எண்ணங்களில் இருந்து விலகி விடும். அல்லது, "பேசுதல்," அஃதாவது, எண்ணங்களில் "நான்" மற்றும் "அடுத்தவர்" இவ்விருவருக்கும் இடையே எப்பொழுதும் பேச்சுவார்த்தை நடைபெறுகிறது. எனவே, மனதுக்குள் "பேசுதலை" நிறுத்தினால், அதாவது, மனதிலிருந்து ஒரு வார்த்தை கூட எழாமல் பார்த்துக் கொண்டால் மற்ற இரண்டு கூறுகளான "நான்" மற்றும் "அடுத்தவர்," எண்ணங்களில் இருந்து விலகி விடுகிறது.

மனம் என்பது படங்களாலும், வார்த்தைகளாலும் ஆனது. அதாவது, ஒளி மற்றும் ஒலி. எண்ணங்களில், "நான்" மற்றும் "அடுத்தவர்" இவ்விரண்டும் படங்களாகும் (ஒளி.) "பேசுதல்" என்பது வார்த்தைகளாகும் (ஒலி.) படங்களும் வார்த்தைகளும் ஒன்றோடு ஒன்று பின்னி பிணைந்துள்ளது. இதன் காரணமாக, இரண்டும் ஒன்றை ஒன்று பரஸ்பரமாக தூண்டிக் கொள்கிறது. இயல்பாகவே, "நான்" "அடுத்தவர்" மற்றும் "பேசுதல்" மனதை எப்பொழுதும் ஊடுருவிக்

கொண்டே தான் இருக்கும். ஆனால், இவைகளில் ஏதாவது ஒன்றை விடா முயற்சி மேற்கொண்டு, தொடர்ச்சியாக மூன்று நிமிடங்களுக்காவது ஒருவர் நிறுத்துவாரேயானால், அது மிகப்பெரிய மேன்மையான நிலையை அவருக்கு நல்கும்.

நீண்ட நெடுங்காலமாக ஒருவர் சுமந்து கொண்டு இருக்கும் தனது முற்கால பாவ வினைகள் எரிந்து சாம்பலாகத் துவங்கும்.

6

பார்ப்பவரும், பார்க்கப்படுவதும்

இந்த பிரபஞ்சத்தின் “மூலம்” மற்றும் அதன் அற்புதமான இயக்கம் பற்றிய உண்மைகளை கண்டுபிடிக்க விழையும் ஒரு இயற்பியல் விஞ்ஞானி, அதே அற்புதமான இயக்கத்தின் ஒரு அங்கமே ஆவார். மரங்கள், மலர்கள், மலைகள், பள்ளத்தாக்கு, விண்மீன்கள், பற்பல உயிரினங்கள் போன்ற இயற்கையின் அற்புதத்தையும் அழகையும் காணும் ஒரு மனிதர், அதே இயற்கையைச் சார்ந்தவரே.

இப்பிரபஞ்சத்தின் உண்மையை அறிய ஒரு அணுவின் மையக்கருவை கண்டறிய முற்படும் ஒரு இயற்பியல் விஞ்ஞானி, கண்டறிய முற்படும் அந்த மையக்கருவில் இருந்து மாறுபட்டவர் அல்ல. பகுப்பாய்வு செய்யப்படும் ஒரு அணுவின் உள் இயங்கும்அதேமையக்கருவே,பகுப்பாய்வுசெய்யும் அந்த விஞ்ஞானியின் உள்ளும் இயங்குகிறது. இரண்டு மையக்கருவும் வெவ்வேறானது இல்லை. எனவே, "பார்ப்பவரும்" "பார்க்கப்படுவதும்" ஒன்றே. ஆராய்ச்சி செய்பவரும், ஆராயப்படுவதும் ஒன்றே.

ஒரு நடைமுறை விளக்கத்திற்காக பார்த்தோமேயானால், ஒரு கவிஞரையும் அவர் எழுதிய கவிதையையும் தனித்தனியே பார்க்க இயலும். அது போலவே, ஒரு ஓவியரையும் அவர் வரைந்த ஓவியத்தையும் தனித்தனியே பார்க்க முடியும். ஒரு இசையமைப்பாளரையும் அவர் அமைத்த இசையையும் தனித்தனியே கண்டுகொள்ள இயலும். ஆனால், நடனத்தையும், நடனமிடுபவரையும் தனித்தனியே காண இயலாது. நடனத்தின் அழகே, அதை, நடனம் ஆடுபவரிடத்தில் இருந்து பிரித்து காணல் இயலாது. நடனம் ஆடுபவர் நின்றால், நடனமும் நின்றுவிடும். நடனத்தை பார்ப்பது, நடனம் ஆடுபவரையும் பார்த்தல் ஆகும்.

இதைப் போன்றே, இந்த முழு பிரபஞ்சத்தின் இயக்கமும், ஒரு புனித நடனமாகும். இதில், நடனம் ஆடுபவர் நடனத்திலிருந்து தனித்து நிற்கவில்லை. அசைப்பவரை காண, அசைவை காண வேண்டும். இப்பிரபஞ்ச அசைவில் நாமும் ஓர் அங்கம் என்பதால், நமது சுய அசைவுகளைப் பார்ப்பதே, அசைக்கும் மூலவரின் தரிசனத்தை பெறும் மார்க்கம் ஆகும். புறப்பொருளை பகுப்பாய்வு செய்ய புலன்கள் பயன்படுத்தப் படுவதால், கண்டறியப்படும் அவ்வுண்மை புலன்களுக்கு உட்பட்டதே அன்றி, புலன்களையே இயக்கிக் கொண்டிருக்கும் மைய உண்மையாக இராது. எனவே, கண்களால் பார்க்கப்படுவது எதுவாயினும், காதுகளால் கேட்கப்படுவது எதுவாயினும், நுகர்வது மற்றும் தொட்டு உணர்வது எதுவாயினும், அது மூலத்திற்கெல்லாம் மூலம் ஆகாது. ஆழ்ந்த உறக்கத்தில், புலன்கள் செயலற்று இருக்கிறது. “நான்” எனப்படும் ஜீவன், நனவில் மட்டும் இருக்கும் ஒரு வஸ்து அல்ல. கனவு மற்றும் ஆழ்ந்த உறக்கத்திலும் “நான்” என்ற ஜீவனின் இருத்தல் உள்ளது. “மூலத்தின்” இருப்பு, புலன்களைத் தாண்டிய ஆழ்ந்த உறக்க நிலையிலும் இருப்பதால், நனவு நிலையில் புலன்களை மட்டுமே வைத்து செய்யப்படும் “மூலம்” பற்றிய ஆய்வு முழுமையானதாக ஆகாது.

ஆழ்ந்த உறக்கத்தில், "பார்ப்பவரும்" "பார்க்கப்படுவதும்" இருக்கவில்லை. உறக்கத்தில் இருந்து விழிக்கும் போது, "பார்ப்பவர்" எப்போதும் "பார்க்ப்படுவது" கூடவே விழிக்கிறார். எனவே, "பார்ப்பவர்," "பார்க்ப்படுவதிலிருந்து" எக்கணத்திலும் தனியாக இல்லை. ஒருவரின் உண்மையான இருப்பு நிலை என்பது, "பார்ப்பவர்," "பார்க்ப்படுவது" என்ற நிலையிலிருந்து தனியாக சுயமாக உள்ளது என்பது ஆழ்ந்த உறக்க நிலையை துல்லியமாகவும், சரியான முறையில் ஒப்பிட்டு பார்ப்பதன் மூலமாகவும் தெரிய வருகிறது. "பார்ப்பவர்" மற்றும் "பார்க்கப்படுவது," சுயத்தை அல்லது "மூலத்தை" மறைக்கும் திரையாகவே விளங்குகிறது.

அடிப்படையில், "பார்த்தல்" என்பது யாது? ஒரு மலரை ஒருவர் பார்க்கும் போது, பார்ப்பவர் "நான்" எனவும், பார்க்கப்படுவது "மலர்" எனவும் ஆகிறது.

"நான்" மலரை பார்க்கிறது. பார்க்கும் அந்த தருணத்தில், பார்ப்பவர் எந்த இடத்தில் முடிந்து, பார்க்கப்படுவது எந்த இடத்தில் இருந்து தொடங்குகிறது? எந்தக் கோடு பார்ப்பவரை ஒரு பக்கமும், பார்க்கப்படுவதை மறு பக்கமும் பிரித்து வரையறுக்கிறது? பார்க்கப்படும் அந்த தருணத்தில், "பார்ப்பவர்" மற்றும் "பார்க்கப்படுவது" இவற்றிற்கிடையில் எந்த இடத்தில் பிரிவு உள்ளது? "பார்ப்பவர்" "பார்க்கப்படுவது" என்ற பிரிவு இல்லாமல் "பார்த்தல்" என்ற நிகழ்வு மட்டுமே நடைபெறுகிறது.

உதாரணமாக, ஒரு நிலைக்கண்ணாடி, அதன் முன்னே தோன்றும் எதையும் பிரதிபலிக்கிறது. நிலை கண்ணாடி எப்பொழுதும் பிரதிபலிக்கும் வேலையை மட்டுமே செய்கிறது. பிரதிபலிக்கும்

தன்மையை நிலைக்கண்ணாடியால் தவிர்க்கவே இயலாது. இதைப் போன்றே, “பார்ப்பவர்” பார்க்ப்படுவதில் இருந்து விலகவே முடியாது. நிலை கண்ணாடியைப் போல, “பார்ப்பவர்” மலரை பிரதிபலிக்கிறார். இங்கே, நிலை கண்ணாடிக்கு நினைவுகளோ அல்லது ஞாபகசக்தியோ இல்லை. எனவே அது நிகழ்காலத்தில் அதன் முன்னே நிகழ்பவைகளை மட்டுமே பிரதிபலிக்கிறது. ஆனால் மனிதன் என்ற “பார்ப்பவருக்கு,” ஞாபகங்கள் என்ற ஒன்று இயங்குவதால், சென்ற காலத்தில் தான் பிரதிபலித்ததையும் தன் மீது நினைவுகளாக படரச் செய்துள்ளார். “பார்ப்பவர்” என்பவர், சென்ற காலம் மற்றும் நிகழ் காலத்தில் “பார்க்கப்பட்டவை”களின் தொகுப்பே ஆவார். இதுமட்டுமின்றி, பார்ப்பவரின் கண்களில் நிறத்தை அறிவதில் குறைபாடு இருந்தால், அவர் அந்த மலரை கருப்பு வெள்ளையாகத் தான் பார்க்க இயலும். அது மட்டுமல்லாமல் தனது இரு கண்களையும் புருவ மத்தியில் நிறுத்தி மலரைப் பார்த்தால், அந்த மலர் இரண்டு மலர்களாகத் தெரியும். பார்க்கப்படுவது அனைத்தும் பார்ப்பவரின் கண்கள் மற்றும் மூளையின் வரையறுக்கப்பட்ட அம்சங்களே ஆகும். உதாரணத்திற்கு, வேறொரு உயர் சக்தி படைத்த ஜீவன் அதே மலரைப் பார்த்தால், ஒருவேளை

அந்த மலர் முற்றிலும் வேறு நிறத்திலும், வேறு வடிவத்திலும் கூட காட்சி அளிக்கலாம். ஒரு புரிதலுக்காக பார்த்தோமேயானால், ஒருவேளை பார்ப்பவருக்கு வடிவங்களை அறிவதில் மூளையில் குறைபாடு இருக்குமேயானால், அந்த மலரின் வடிவம் முற்றிலும் வேறு உருவத்தில் தென்படும் அல்லது அந்த மலரே தென்படாமலும் இருக்கக்கூடும். நம் மூளை அல்லது மனதில் ஏற்கனவே, நிபந்தனைக்குட்பட்டு, வரையறுக்கப்பட்டு உள்ளவைகளைத் தான் நாம் புறத்தில் பார்த்துக் கொண்டு இருக்கிறோம். பார்ப்பவரே பார்க்கப்படும் மலருக்கு நிறத்தையும் வடிவத்தையும் அளித்து அதனை பார்க்கப்படும் ஒரு பொருளாகப் பார்க்கிறார். பார்ப்பவரே பார்க்கப்படுவதை அவ்விதமாக படைக்கிறார். பார்க்கப்படும் காட்சி, பார்ப்பவர் இடத்தில் இருந்தே தோன்றுகிறது. பார்ப்பவர் இல்லை என்றால் “பார்க்கப்படுவதும்” இல்லை. மலருக்கு நிறத்தை அளிப்பது பார்ப்பவரே; மலருக்கு வடிவத்தை அளிப்பதும் பார்ப்பவரே. அந்த மலர் அவ்வாறு காட்சியளிக்க “பார்ப்பவரே” காரணம். எனவே, “பார்ப்பவரே” புறத்தில் தோன்றும் அந்த மலரின் காட்சியும் ஆவார். மரம், செடி கொடிகள் மற்றும் பார்க்கப்படும் இந்த முழு பிரபஞ்சமும் மனம் என்ற பார்ப்பவரிடத்தில் இருந்து வெளிப்படும்

காட்சியே. பார்ப்பவரும் “பார்க்கப்படுவதும்” ஒன்றே ஆகும். மனமே இப்பிரபஞ்சம் ஆகும்.

ஒரு கண்ணாடியின் மேற்பரப்பில், பிரதிபலிப்பை உண்டாக்கிக் கொண்டிருக்கும் மென்படலத்தை நீக்கிவிட்டால், பிரதிபலிப்பு முற்றிலும் நீங்கிவிடுகிறது. நீக்கப்பட்ட அந்த மென்படலத்தை இதுநாள் வரை தன் மேற்பரப்பில் தாங்கி பிடித்துக் கொண்டு இருந்தது எதுவோ, அதுவே அந்த மொத்த பிரதிபலிப்பின் ஆதாரம் அல்லது “மூலம்” ஆகும். இதைப் போன்றே, ஒரு மனிதருள் உலகை பிரதிபலித்துக் கொண்டிருக்கும் ஐம்புலன்களை கொண்ட மனம் என்ற கண்ணாடியை, தன் மேற்பரப்பில் தாங்கி கொண்டிருப்பது எதுவோ, அதுவே “பார்ப்பவரின்” ஆதாரம் அல்லது “மூலம்” ஆகும். ஒரு மனிதரிடத்தில் “பார்ப்பவர்” மற்றும் “பார்க்கப்படுவது” என்ற பிரதிபலிப்பு முற்றிலும் நீங்கியிருக்கும் தருணம், “ஆழ்ந்த உறக்கம்” ஆகும். அந்த ஆழ்ந்த உறக்கத்தில் “வாழ்ந்து கொண்டிருப்பது” எதுவோ, அதுவே இந்த பிரபஞ்சம் மற்றும் அனைத்து உயிரினங்களின் மையக்கரு, ஆதாரம் அல்லது மூலத்திற்கெல்லாம் மூலம் ஆகும். ஒருவர், தனக்கே பிரத்யேகமாக உண்டானதான மற்றும் தனது இயல்புக்கு பொருந்தக் கூடிய உரிய மார்க்கத்தின்

மூலமாக, தனது முழு விழிப்பு நிலையில், “பார்ப்பவர்” “பார்க்கப்படுவது” எனப்படுவதை முற்றிலுமாக குறிப்பிட்ட கால அளவிற்கு நீக்குவாரேயானால், அனைத்திற்கும் மூலமான “மூலவர்” அறியப்படுகிறார்.

7

தன்னுணர்வு

நீங்கள் ஒரு வாகனத்தில் பயணம் செய்யும் போது, அந்த வாகனத்தின் நகர்வை உங்களது நகர்வு என கூற இயலுமா?

வாகனம்தான் நகர்கிறதே தவிர, நீங்கள் இல்லை. வாகனத்தின் நகர்வு மற்றும் அது திரும்பும் திசைக்கு ஏற்ப, நாம் பல காட்சிகளை காண்கிறோம். இதைப் போன்றே, நீங்கள் ஓரிடத்தில் இருந்து மற்றொரு இடத்திற்கு நடந்து செல்கையில்,

உண்மையில் நீங்கள் நகர்கின்றீர்களா அல்லது உங்கள் உடல் நகர்கின்றதா? உங்கள் உடல் தலைகீழாக நின்றால், நீங்கள் தலைகீழாகவா உள்ளீர்கள்? அதாவது, உடல் தலைகீழாக நிற்கும் பொழுது,உங்கள்"நான்"என்றஉணர்வுதலைகீழாக உள்ளதா? உட்காருதல், நடத்தல், ஓடுதல், சாய்தல், சுற்றுதல் போன்ற உடலின் பல்வேறு நிலைகளிலும் உங்கள் "நான்" எனப்படுவது ஒரே மாதிரியாகத்தானே இருக்கிறது? உங்களின் குழந்தைப் பருவம் முதல் முதுமைப் பருவம் வரை, உடலின் தோற்றம் மாறும் போதும், எண்ணங்கள் மாறும் போதும், கண்ணோட்டம் மாறும் போதும், "நான்" என்ற தன்னுணர்வு மட்டும் மாறாமல், ஒரே வகையாக, ஒரே தன்மையுடன் அல்லவா தொடர்ந்து உடன் வருகிறது?

கண்களை மூடி ஒரு சில விநாடிகள் மூச்சை நிறுத்தி "நான்" என்ற அந்த தன்னுணர்வை கவனித்தால், அது ஒரு மௌனமான விழிப்புணர்வு என்பதை உணரலாம். அந்த மௌனமான விழிப்புணர்வுதான் எந்த வித அசைவோ நகர்வோ இன்றி சிறு வயது முதல் தற்போது வரை உங்களுடனேயே இருந்து வருகிறது.

கண்களை மூடி மூச்சு உள் வரும்போதோ அல்லது வெளியில் செல்லும் போதோ மூன்று அல்லது நான்கு விநாடிகளுக்கு அதனை நிறுத்தி, உங்கள் "நான்" என்ற தன்னுணர்வை கவனிக்க வேண்டும். "நான்" என்ற தன்னுணர்வை கவனித்துக் கொண்டே மூச்சினை எப்போதும் போல் இயங்க விட்டுவிட வேண்டும். "நான்" என்ற தன்னுணர்வோடு சிறிது நேரம் இவ்வாறு இருக்கும் போது, அது ஒரு ஆழமான அமைதி பொருந்திய வர்ணிக்க முடியாத விழிப்புணர்வு நிலை என்பதும், அது, அசைவுகளுக்கும், நகர்வுகளுக்கும்

அப்பாற்பட்டது என்பதனையும், ஒரு குறிப்பிட்ட வடிவத்திலோ அல்லது உருவத்திலோ அது இல்லை என்பதனையும் உணர்ந்து கொள்ள முடியும். ஒரு வடிவம் அல்லது உருவம் தான், ஓரிடத்தில் இருந்து இன்னோர் இடத்திற்கு நகர முடியும் அல்லது இருந்த இடத்தில் இருந்து அசைவை ஏற்படுத்த முடியும். மேலும், ஒரு வடிவம் அல்லது உருவத்திற்குத் தான், “உள்ளே” மற்றும் “வெளியே” என்ற நிலைகள் உண்டு. ஒருவரின் உண்மையான “நான்”ஆக விளங்கும் இந்த மகா மௌனமான தன்னுணர்வு கொண்ட விழிப்புணர்வு, வடிவத்திற்கும் உருவத்திற்கும் அப்பாற்பட்டது என்பதனால், அதற்கு “உள்ளே” என்ற ஒரு நிலை இல்லை. “உள்ளே” என்ற நிலை அதற்கு இல்லாமையால் “வெளியே” என்ற நிலையும் அதற்கு கிடையாது. ஏனெனில், “உள்ளே” மற்றும் “வெளியே” என்ற இரு நிலைகளும் ஒரு உருவத்தை மையமாக வைத்து, அந்த உருவத்தின் கோணத்தில் இருந்து உரைக்கப்படும் வார்த்தைகளாகும். அகமும் புறமும் அற்ற அந்த விழிப்புணர்வு, உண்மையில் ஒருவரின் உடலுக்கு உள்ளே இல்லை. உடல் தான் அதன் மேல் உள்ளது. உடலின் கோணத்தில் இருந்து பார்க்கும் போது, இந்த விழிப்புணர்வு, “உள்ளே” உள்ளது. இந்த விழிப்புணர்வின் நிலைப்பாட்டில் இருந்து

பார்க்கும் போது, உடலானது அதன் மேல் உள்ளது. திரையரங்கில் ஒளிபரப்பப்படும் திரைப்படம், வெள்ளைத் துணியில் ஒளிபரப்பப்படுகிறது. திரைப்படத்தில் உலா வரும் மாய கதாநாயகனின் நிலைப்பாட்டில் இருந்து பார்க்கும் போது, வெள்ளைத் துணி, அந்த திரைப்படத்திற்கு “உள்ளே” உள்ளது. ஆனால், நகராமல் விளங்கும் வெள்ளைத் துணியின் நிலைப்பாட்டில் இருந்து பார்க்கும் போது, மாறிக்கொண்டே இருக்கும் காட்சிகளை கொண்ட அந்த திரைப்படம், அதன் மேற்பரப்பில் உள்ளது. கனவில் ஒருவர் ஒரு மரத்தை கண்டு அதை நோக்கி நடந்து சென்று அதனை தொடுகிறார். விழித்தவுடன், அந்த மரம், தனது உடல், இரண்டிற்கும் இடையில் இருந்த இடைவெளி, அந்த மரத்தை தொட எடுத்துக் கொண்ட கால அளவு மற்றும் தூரம், அந்த மரத்தை தொடும் பொழுது ஏற்பட்ட உணர்வு ஆகிய அனைத்தும், தூக்கத்தின் காரணமாக விழிப்புணர்வு வெளிப்படுத்திய மாய காட்சி என்பதனை தெரிந்து கொள்கிறார். இதைப் போன்றே, பிரபஞ்சத்தில் பார்க்கப்படும் வெட்டவெளி, நட்சத்திரங்கள், கிரகங்கள், உயிரினங்கள், நடக்கும் நிகழ்வுகள் அனைத்தும் “நான்” என தன்னுணர்வுடன் விளங்கும் நித்திய மௌனம் பொருந்திய ஓர் மகா விழிப்புணர்வில் இருந்து வெளிப்படும்

காட்சிகளாகும். பார்க்கப்படும் அனைத்தும் விழிப்புணர்வில் இருந்து வெளிவருவதால், அனைத்தும் விழிப்புணர்வே ஆகும். அனைத்தும் விழிப்புணர்வே என்பதால், இந்த விழிப்புணர்வுக்கு இரட்டை தன்மை இல்லை. இருப்பது ஒரே ஒரு விழிப்புணர்வே. ஒவ்வொருவர்க்கு உள்ளும் வசிக்கும் இந்த "நான்" என்ற விழிப்புணர்வு ஒன்றே ஆகும். தன்னுணர்வு என்பது அனைவருக்கும் ஒன்றே. அனைத்து ஜீவன்களுக்கும் "தன்னுணர்வு" என்பது வெவ்வேறாக இருப்பது இல்லை. எவ்வாறு, வெற்றிடம் வீட்டின் உள்ளே மற்றும் வீட்டின் வெளியே பரந்து விளங்குகிறதோ, அவ்வாறே, இந்த மகா விழிப்புணர்வு அனைத்து உடல்களின் உள்ளும் மற்றும் வெளியிலும் எல்லையற்று பரந்து விளங்குகின்றது. நான்கு சுவர்களால் சூழப்பட்ட வெற்றிடம் வீடு எனவும், களிமண்ணால் சூழப்பட்ட வெற்றிடம் பானையாகவும் எவ்வாறு கருதப்படுகிறதோ, அது போலவே, மனித உடலால் சூழப்பட்ட இந்த விழிப்புணர்வு மனிதனாகவும், மிருக உடலால் சூழப்பட்ட இந்த விழிப்புணர்வு மிருகமாகவும், இதுபோல பறவைகளாகவும், செடி கொடி, புழுக்கள் பூச்சுகளாகவும், ஞாயிறும் சந்திரனுமாக தாமே விளங்குகிறது.

ஒரு மனித உடலில், நனவில் தலைப் பகுதியில் இயங்கும் மனம், கனவில் தொண்டை

பகுதியில் இயங்கும் மனம், ஆழ்ந்த உறக்கத்தில் மார்பு பகுதியில் அடங்கும் மனம், இந்த மகா விழிப்புணர்வு கடலின் கட்டுப்பாட்டில் இயங்கும் ஒரு சிறு நீர் குமிழி ஆகும்.

8

விதி

ஒரு தொலைக்காட்சி பெட்டியில், ஒளிப்படக் குழாய், தாய்ப்பலகை, கேளொலி அமைப்பு, அலைவாங்கி, காட்சித்திரை போன்ற மேலும் எண்ணற்ற பாகங்கள் அடங்கியுள்ளது. ஒரு காணொளி, வேறொரு இடத்திலிருந்து தொலைக்காட்சி பெட்டியின் வழியாக ஒளிபரப்பப் படுகிறது. ஒரு காணொளியில், ஒளி மற்றும் ஒலி தடையின்றி சீராக தொலைக்காட்சி பெட்டியில் வெளிப்பட வேண்டுமெனில், அந்த தொலைக்காட்சி பெட்டியின் உள் பாகங்கள் சரியாகவும் முறையாகவும் பழுதின்றி செயல்பட வேண்டும். ஏதேனும் ஓர் முக்கிய பகுதி பழுதடைந்து செயல்படவில்லையெனில் காணொளி திரையில் வெளிப்படாது. காணொளி ஒளிபரப்பப் படுவதில் தொலைக்காட்சி பெட்டியின் உள் பாகங்கள் மிக முக்கிய பங்கு வகிக்கின்ற காரணத்தினால், அந்த உள் பாகங்களில் இருந்து தான் காணொளி தோன்றி திரையில் ஒளிபரப்பாகிறது என்று பொருளில்லை. ஒளியும் ஒலியும் கலந்த காணொளி, வேறொர் இடத்தில் இருந்து தொலைக்காட்சி

பெட்டியின் உள் பாகங்கள் வழியாக திரையில் ஒளிபரப்பப் படுகிறது. ஒரு குறிப்பிட்ட காணொளி ஒளிபரப்பாக, தொலைக்காட்சி பெட்டி ஒரு ஊடகமே ஆகும்.

ஒருவருடைய இதயம், மூளை மற்றும் அனைத்து உடல் உறுப்புகளும் தொலைக்காட்சி பெட்டியின் பாகங்கள் போலத்தான். எண்ணமும் பேச்சும், உடல் பாகங்களை பயன்படுத்தி அதன் வழியாக அல்லது ஊடாக, உறுப்புகளைத் தாண்டிய ஓர் இடத்தில் இருந்து வெளிப்படுவதே அன்றி, உடலின் உள் உறுப்புகளில் இருந்து ஆரம்பிப்பது இல்லை. ஒருவரின் மூளையில் ஒரு விஷயம் எவ்வாறு, எந்த தாக்கத்துடன் பதிய வேண்டும் என்பதும், பதிந்த அவ் விஷயங்களை எப்போது எவ்வாறு பயன்படுத்த வேண்டும் என்பதும், மற்றும் மூளையில் இருந்து வெளிப்படும் அனைத்து நுட்பமான செயல்பாடுகளும், மூளை தாமாக செய்கின்ற வேளை போல் காட்சி அளித்தாலும், மூளை அதை தாமாக செய்வதில்லை. மூளையை ஒரு கருவியாக பயன்படுத்தி உயர் சக்தியே அதனை இயக்குகிறது.

உடல் என்பது வெவ்வேறாக பல கோடிகள் இருந்தாலும், அனைத்து உடல்களின் தன்மையும் ஒன்றே. நிறம், உயரம், வடிவம் ஆகியவைகளில்

மாற்றம் இருப்பினும், அனைத்து உடல்களின் இயல்பும் தரமும் ஒன்றே ஆகும். ஒரு தனி உடலைப் பற்றிய ஒரு கண்டுபிடிப்பு, அனைத்து உடலைகளைப் பற்றிய கண்டுபிடிப்பாகும். ஒரு உடல் குணமடைய கண்டுபிடிக்கப்பட்ட ஓர் மருந்து, அனைத்து உடல்களும் குணமடைய கண்டுபிடிக்கப்பட்ட மருந்தாகும். அனைத்து உடல்களும் ஒரே அம்சத்தைக் கொண்டதே. மனதின் அம்சமும் அவ்வாறே. பல்வேறு விதமான மனங்கள் இருந்தாலும், அனைத்து மனங்களின் தன்மையும் ஒன்றே. அச்சம் கொண்ட ஒருவரின் மனம் எவ்வாறு சிந்திக்க துவங்குமோ, அதே தன்மையில் தான் அனைவரின் மனங்களும் சிந்திக்கும்.

விளக்கில் எரியும் ஒரு தீபத்திடமிருந்து பல கோடி விளக்குகள் அந்த தீபத்தை தனது திரியில் ஏற்றிக்கொண்டு தனித்தனியே உலகின் வெவ்வேறு இடத்தில் வாழ்ந்தாலும், அனைத்திலும் எரியும் தீபம் ஒன்றே. பல்வேறு விதமான தோற்றங்கள் கொண்ட அனைத்து விளக்குகளிலும் எரிந்து கொண்டிருக்கும் தீபம், ஒரே தீபம் ஆகும். அந்த தீபத்தினைப் போன்றே, அனைத்து உயிரினங்களுக்கு உள்ளும் நிலவும் “நான்” என்ற தன்னுணர்வு, வெவ்வேறான, பலவகையான தன்னுணர்வு இல்லை. இருப்பது

ஒரே ஒரு தன்னுணர்வு மட்டுமே. “அடுத்தவர்” என நாம் யாரை குறிப்பிடுகிறோமோ, அவர் அவரை “நான்” என்று தான் குறிப்பிடுகிறார். “நீ,” “அவர்” என்பதெல்லாம் வெறும் சொற்கூறுகளே. அனைத்தும் “நான்”ஆகவே இருக்கிறது. அந்த “நான்” என்பது ஒரே “நான்” தான். உடலில் ஏற்படும் ஒரு வலியின் உணர்வு எவ்வாறு அனைவருக்கும் ஒரே உணர்வு ஆகுமோ, மகிழ்ச்சி என்ற உணர்வு எவ்வாறு அனைவருக்கும் ஒரே உணர்வு ஆகுமோ, “நான்” என்ற தன்னைப் பற்றிய உணர்வும் அனைவருக்கும் ஒன்றே ஆகும். இந்த ஒரே ஒரு தன்னுணர்வு தான், அனைத்து உடல்களிலும் இருந்து கொண்டு உடலின் பாகங்கள் வாயிலாகவும், மனதின் வாயிலாகவும், சிந்தனைகளையும் செயல்களையும் தூண்டி, உலக நிகழ்வுகளை நிகழ்த்துகிறது. அனைத்து உடல்களில் இருந்து செயல்களைத் தூண்டுவது ஒரே ஒரு தன்னுணர்வு மட்டுமே என்பதால், ஒரு சிறு அசைவு முதற்கொண்டு, ஒரு தனி மனிதன் ஒவ்வொரு தருணமும் பெறும் அனுபவங்கள் உட்பட உலக நிகழ்வுகள் யாவும் தீர்மானிக்கப்பட்டு, நிர்ணயிக்கப்பட்டு நடக்கின்றனவே அன்றி, தற்செயலாக நடப்பது அறவே அன்று. உதாரணத்திற்கு, ஒரு மனிதர் ஒரு பூங்காவில் தனது பாலிய நண்பரை எதிர்பாராத

விதமாக திடீரென சந்திக்கிறார் என்றால், அந்த பூங்காவிற்கு அந்த குறிப்பிட்ட நேரத்தில் இவரை செல்லத் தூண்டியது, இவரின் "நான்" ஆகும். இது போன்றே, அந்த குறிப்பிட்ட நேரத்தில் அதே பூங்காவிற்கு இவரது நண்பரை செல்லத் தூண்டியது அவரது "நான்" ஆகும்.

இருவரின் மனதை பொருத்தமட்டில், அந்த சந்திப்பு எதேச்சையானது. ஆனால், ஒவ்வொருவரின் மனதிற்கு பின்னால் இருக்கும் தன்னுணர்வான "நான்"ஐ பொருத்தமட்டில், அந்த நிகழ்வு நிச்சயிக்கப்பட்ட ஒரு நிகழ்வாகும்.

இருவரையும் அந்த பூங்காவிற்கு அழைத்துச் சென்றது, ஒரே "நான்" தான். நம்முடைய மனமும் உடலும் தான் தனித்தனியாக, வெவ்வேறாக இருக்கிறதே அன்றி, "நான்" என்ற தன்னுணர்வு இல்லை. நாம் நமது மனதுடனும் உடலுடனும் மட்டுமே நம்மை அடையாளப் படுத்திக் கொண்டு உள்ளமையால், நம்மை தனி நபர்களாக உணர்கிறோம். நமது மனமானது சிந்தித்துக் கொண்டிருக்கவில்லை, எண்ணங்களை பெற்றுக் கொண்டு மட்டுமே இருக்கிறது. ஒரு இரும்புத் துண்டு தானே நகர்ந்து செல்வதாக கருதிக் கொண்டாலும், கண்ணிற்கு புலப்படாத காந்த சக்தியே அதனை நகர்த்துகிறது. ஒவ்வொரு நொடியும், உலக உயிரினங்களின் அனைத்து மனதையும் தூண்டி, அனைத்து நிகழ்வுகளையும், தான் விதித்தவாறே நிகழ்த்துவது இந்த ஒற்றை "நானே" ஆகும். தன்னுணர்வு என்பது ஒன்றே என்பதாலும், அதைத் தாண்டிய இன்னொரு இரண்டாம் வஸ்து இல்லை என்பதாலும், உலகில் நடப்பவை அனைத்தும் முன்கூட்டியே தீர்மானிக்கப்பட்டு, விதிக்கப்பட்டவைகளே ஆகும். இந்த தன்னுணர்வு, "நான்" என்ற உணர்வோடு வீற்றிருக்கவில்லை. "நான்" என்று அடுத்தவரிடத்தில் தான் கூற முடியும். அந்த அடுத்துவரும் இந்த "நான்" தான் எனும்போது,

யாரிடத்தில் அது தன்னை "நான்" என கூற முடியும்? அடுத்தவர் என ஒருவர் இருந்தால் தான், நான் என்ற எண்ணமே எழும். அதன் முன்னால் இருப்பதும் அதுவே என்பதால், "நான்" என்ற உணர்வோடு, அந்த மகா விழிப்புணர்வு வீற்றிருக்கவில்லை.

ஒரு மரத்தின் வடிவம், உயரம், ஆழம் மற்றும் அதன் தன்மை முழுவதையும் அது மரமாக வளர்வதற்கு முன்னதாகவே, அதன் விதையினுள் தீர்மானிக்கப்பட்டு, நிர்ணயிக்கப்பட்டு, பதிக்கப்பட்டுவிட்டது. ஒவ்வொரு நாளும் அந்த விதையானது வளரும் போது, ஏற்கனவே தீர்மானிக்கப்பட்ட, வடிவமைக்கப்பட்ட, விதிக்கப்பட்ட அம்சங்களுடனும் தன்மைகளுடனும் தான் வளர முடியுமே தவிர, அதிலிருந்து மீள இயலாது. ஒரு தென்னங்கன்று மாயிலைகளையும் மாம்பழத்தையும் வெளிக் கொணர இயலாது. அது போலவே, அனைத்து மனிதர்கள் மற்றும் உயிரினங்களின் வாழ்வும் எதிர்கொள்கின்ற அனுபவங்களும் முன்கூட்டியே தீர்மானிக்கப்பட்டு விதிக்கப்பட்டவையே ஆகும். மரத்தினை விதை வெளிக்கொணர்வதைப் போல, ஒவ்வொரு நாளும் நாம் நமக்கு விதிக்கப்பட்டவையையே எதிர்கொள்கிறோம்.

ஒரு ஞானியும் அவரது பத்து சீடர்களும் ஒரு காட்டின் வழியே பக்கத்து கிராமத்திற்கு சில மூலிகைகள் வாங்க சென்று கொண்டிருந்தனர். காட்டின் வழியே பயணிக்கையில், ஓரிடத்தில் ஒரு சிறிய, அழகான, சிறிது இலைகளையே துளிர்த்திருந்த ஓர் செடியைக் கண்டனர். ஞானியிடத்தில் எப்பொழுதும் வாக்குவாதம் செய்யும் பழக்கமுடைய ஒரு சீடன், அந்த செடியின் அருகில் நின்று "குருவே! இந்த அழகான செடி பெரிய மரமாக வளர்ந்து பல வருடங்கள் வாழும் விதியை பெற்றிருக்கிறதா" என ஞானியிடம் வினவினான். ஞானி அந்த செடியின் அருகே கண்களை மூடி அமர்ந்தார். சிறிது நேரம் கழித்து கண்களை திறந்து "ஆம்! இந்த சிறிய செடி பெரிய மரமாக வளர்ந்து நீண்டகாலம் வாழும் விதியைப் பெற்றிருக்கிறது" என்று அச்சீடனுக்கு பதிலளித்தார். அவரின் பதிலைக் கேட்ட மறுகணமே அந்த சீடன், அந்த செடியை வேரோடு பிடுங்கி எறிந்தான். மேலும், பலத்த சிரிப்புடன் "பார்த்தீர்களா குருவே! நான் உங்கள் கூற்றை தவறாக்கிவிட்டேன். உங்கள் ஞான திரிஷ்டியில் இந்த செடியின் விதியினைப் பற்றி நீங்கள் அறிந்து கொண்டது உங்களின் கற்பனையே. விதி என ஒன்று எவருக்கும் இல்லை. அனைத்தும் தற்செயலாக நடைபெறுவதே" என வலுவான தன் வாதத்தினை முன்வைத்தான்.

ஞானி பதில் ஏதும் உரைக்காமல் மௌனமாக பயணத்தை தொடர ஆரம்பித்தார். பொழுது சாயும் வேளையில், அனைவரும் அடுத்த கிராமத்தில் உள்ள ஓர் ஆசிரமத்தை சென்றடைந்தனர். குருவை வெற்றிகொண்ட அந்த சீடன், தனது பெருமையை மற்ற சீடர்களுடன் மீண்டும் மீண்டும் பகிர்ந்து மகிழலானான். அன்றிரவு முழுவதும் திடீரென பலத்த மழை பொழிந்தது. மறு நாளும் மழை தொடர்ந்து பொழியவே, வெளியில் எங்கும் செல்லாமல் அனைவரும் ஆசிரமத்திலேயே தங்கிவிட்டனர். இரண்டாம் நாள் காலையில் மழை நின்றவுடன், கிராமத்தில் தமக்கு தேவையான அனைத்து மூலிகைகளையும் வாங்கிக் கொண்டு தமது சொந்த கிராமத்திற்கு அதே காட்டின் வழியாக அனைவரும் திரும்பிக் கொண்டிருந்தனர். சில மணி நேர பயணத்திற்கு பிறகு, பிடுங்கி எறியப்பட்ட அந்த செடி இருந்த இடத்திற்கு வந்தவுடன், அனைத்து சீடர்களும் பிரமிப்பில் வாயடைத்து நின்றனர். ஏனெனில், பிடுங்கி எறியப்பட்ட அந்த செடியின் வேர்கள் மீண்டும் மண்ணுக்குள் புதையப்பட்டு, முன்பைவிட பல இலைகள் புதியதாக துளிர்த்திருந்தது. பிடுங்கி எறியப்பட்ட அன்றிரவு பொழிந்த கனத்த மழை, இதன் வேரை மண்ணுக்குள் புதைத்து, மீண்டும் இந்த செடிக்கு வாழ்வளித்திருப்பதை அந்த சீடர்கள் உணர்ந்தனர்.

செடியை பிடுங்கி எறிந்த அந்த சீடன், ஞானியின் பாதங்களை கண்ணீர் மல்க பற்றிக் கொண்டு தான் இழைத்த தவற்றிற்கு மன்னிப்பு வேண்டினான். அருட்புன்னகையோடு அந்த ஞானி கூறினார், "அனைவரும், அனைத்தும் விதி வகுத்த வழியில் மட்டுமே செல்ல இயலும். ஒருவேளை ஏதேனும் பிறழ நேரிட்டால், விதியை காக்க அதிசயங்கள் நிகழ்த்தப் படுகின்றது."

9

துறவு

ஞானிகளையும் துறவிகளையும் பெரிதாக மதிக்கின்ற அரசன் ஒருவன் ஒரு நாட்டில் வாழ்ந்து வந்தார். துறவியர் எவரேனும் எங்காவது வசிக்கிறார்கள் என கேள்வியுற்றால் அக்கணமே, அது அடுத்த ராஜ்ஜியத்தைச் சேர்ந்த ஊராக இருப்பினும், அவரை சந்திக்க தனது பயணத்தை ஓர் புனித பயணமாக எண்ணி அந்த ஞானியின் ஆசியை பெற சிரத்தையுடன் கிளம்பிவிடுவார். ஒரு நாள், ஒரு ஞானி தனது ராஜ்ஜியத்தில் உள்ள ஒரு கோயிலில் அமர்ந்திருக்கிறார் என அந்த அரசர் கேள்வியுற்றார். மிகுந்த ஆர்வத்துடனும் மகிழ்ச்சியுடனும் தனது அரசி மற்றும் அமைச்சர்கள் சூழ அந்த ஞானியை சந்திக்க பயணம் மேற்கொண்டார். நீண்ட தூர பயணத்திற்குப் பிறகு அந்த ஞானி தங்கியிருந்த கோயிலை சென்றடைந்தார். கோயிலில், மூடிய கண்களுடன் அசைவற்று அமைதியாக அமர்ந்திருந்த ஞானியை கண்டார். ஞானி, தனது விழிகளை திறக்கின்ற வரையில் வெகு நேரமாக அமைதியாக

காத்திருந்தார் அரசர். ஒருகட்டத்தில் ஞானியானவர் கண்களை திறந்து எதிரே இருந்த அரசரை கண்டார். அரசர் தனது கைகளை கூப்பி வணங்கி, ஞானியிடத்தில், தன்னுடன் தனது அரண்மனைக்கு வந்து சிறிது காலம் தங்கி தனக்கு ஆன்மீகத்தையும் அறத்தையும் கற்பிக்க வேண்டுமென வேண்டி கேட்டுக் கொண்டார். ஒரு சிறு தயக்கம் கூட காட்டாமல் அரசருடன் அரண்மனைக்குச் செல்ல சம்மதித்தார் ஞானி. அரசர் உட்பட அங்கே இருந்த அரசி மற்றும் அமைச்சர்கள் அனைவரும் சற்றே திகைப்பில் ஆழ்ந்தனர். அரண்மனையில் தங்க உடனே துறவி ஒப்புக்கொள்வார் என அரசர் எதிர்ப்பார்க்கவில்லை. இருந்த போதிலும், அவரை மகிழ்ச்சியுடன் அரண்மனைக்கு அழைத்துச் சென்றார். அரசர், அந்த ஞானிக்கு ஓர் அழகான அறையையும், படுத்துறங்க பஞ்சு மெத்தையையும், பட்டால் நெய்யப்பட்ட ஆடைகளையும், அணிந்து கொள்ள தங்க மற்றும் வைர ஆபரணங்களையும் வழங்கினார். ஞானி இவ்வனைத்தையும் தயக்கமின்றி ஏற்றுக் கொண்டதை கண்ட அரசர் மலைத்து நின்றார். ஏனெனில், தங்க நகைகளையும் பட்டாடைகளையும் அவர் நிராகரிப்பார் என எண்ணியிருந்தார். இந்த துறவி உண்மையிலேயே லௌகீக வாழ்வை துறந்தவரா அல்லது இவர் ஒரு போலியா என்ற சந்தேகம் அரசரின் மனதில் எழ

ஆரம்பித்தது. நாட்கள் செல்ல செல்ல அரசரின் சந்தேகம் அதிகமாகிக் கொண்டே இருந்தது. காரணம், அரண்மனை வாழ்க்கையின் அனைத்து சௌகரியங்களையும் அனுபவித்து வந்தார் அந்த ஞானி. அது மட்டுமின்றி, எப்போதெல்லாம் அரசர் அவரை சந்தித்து ஆன்மீக விஷயங்களைப் பற்றி பேச துவங்கினாலும், அப்போதெல்லாம் அவ்வகை உரையாடல்களை தவிர்த்தே வந்தார் அந்த துறவி. அரசி மற்றும் அமைச்சர்கள், இந்த நபர் ஒரு வேடதாரி, அவரை அரண்மனையில் இருந்து அனுப்பி விடுங்கள் என அரசருக்கு அறிவுரை வழங்கினர். மனதில் தைரியத்தை வரவழைத்துக் கொண்டு அரசர் அந்த ஞானியிடம் சென்று தயக்கத்துடன், சந்தேகம் கொண்டிருக்கும் தன் மனதின் நிலையை வெளிப்படையாக அந்த ஞானியிடத்தில் கூறினார்.

புன்னகைத்தபடியே சாந்தமான குரலில் அந்த ஞானி, "எனது அருமை அரசரே! தாம் ஆன்மீக தேடலில் உண்மையான ஊக்கம் கொண்டுள்ளவராக இருப்பதனால் துறவறத்தின் உண்மைப் பொருளை நிச்சயம் உங்களுக்கு உபதேசித்தல் வேண்டும்." இவ்வாறு கூறிக்கொண்டே, தான் அணிந்து இருந்த தங்க நகைகள் மற்றும் பட்டாடைகளை அகற்றி பழைய கோலத்தில் காட்சி அளித்தார் ஞானி. மேலும், "தங்க

நகைகளை அணிந்து கொண்ட போதிலும், அதையே இழந்த போதிலும் எனது இருதய அமைதிக்கும் மன சமநிலைக்கும் சிறிதளவும் பாதிப்பு இல்லை. நீங்கள் அளித்த அரண்மனை சௌகரியங்கள், பஞ்சு மெத்தை, பட்டாடை, தங்க வைர நகைகளுடன் நான் வாழ்ந்தாலும், அவை எவற்றின் மீதும் நான் எள்ளளவும் பற்று கொள்ளவில்லை. வெளியில் இருக்கும் எதையுமே சாராமல், சுயமாக நிலைத்திருக்கும் நித்திய ஆனந்தத்தை எனக்குள்ளே நான் கண்டுகொண்டமையால், வெளியில் இருந்து எனக்கு "வழங்கப்படுவது" அல்லது "பறிக்கப்படுவது" எதுவும் எனை பாதிப்பதில்லை. அருமை அரசரே! ஆனந்தத்தைப் பெற மனித மனம், நிலையற்ற புற பொருள்களின் மீது பற்று கொள்கிறது. இதன் பிறகு, பற்றியதை இழந்து விடுவோமோ என்ற அச்சம் மனதில் குடியேறுகிறது. பற்றின் விளைவாக அச்சமும், அச்சத்தின் விளைவாக மீண்டும் பொருள்களின் மீது அதீத பற்றும் கைகோர்த்து, இரண்டும் மனதை ஆக்கிரமித்துக் கொள்கிறது. அச்சம் கொண்ட மனம் அமைதி பெறுவதில்லை. அமைதியற்ற மனம் நிம்மதி அடைவதில்லை. நிம்மதியை புறத்தில் தேடி அலைந்து அதில் தோல்வியுற்ற மனமானது, ஒரு கட்டத்தில் நிலையற்றவைகளின் மீது உள்ள பற்றே நிம்மதியின்மைக்கு காரணம்

என்பதனை உணர்ந்து, பற்றை துறக்க முயல்கிறது. பற்றினை துறக்க கடுமையாக முயன்றும் அதில் வெற்றி கொள்ள முடியாத மனம், ஒரு கட்டத்தில், பற்றின்மை என்பது நாம் விரும்பி செய்யும் ஒரு செயல் அல்ல, நாம் முயற்சித்து அடையும் ஓர் நிலை அல்ல, பற்றற்ற நிலை என்பது தாமாக ஒருவர்க்கு நிகழும் “விளைவு” என்பதனை புரிந்து கொள்கிறது. எதன் காரணத்தால் பற்றின்மை ஒரு “விளைவாக” ஒருவர்க்கு நிகழ்கிறது என்ற சரியான தேடலின் போது, நிலையானது எதுவோ, அந்த நிலையானதை பற்றும் போது, நிலையற்றவைகளின் மீதான பற்று தாமாகவே அகன்று விடுகிறது என்ற உண்மை அந்த மனதிற்கு உணர்த்தப் படுகிறது. அதன் பிற்பாடு, ஆழ்ந்த ஆய்வுக்குப் பின், ஆழ்ந்த உறக்கத்திலும் தன்னுள் உயிரோடு வசிக்கும் “நான்” என்ற வஸ்துவே என்றும் நிலையானது என்ற உண்மையை மனம் உணர்ந்து கொள்கிறது. எண்ணங்கள் எனும் ஓயாத சலனத்தை முறியடித்து, உடலானது உறங்கும் நிலையிலும் அகத்தின் ஆழத்தில் உள்ள தன்னுணர்வு ஜோதியை, தன் மனோபாவத்திற்கு உரித்தான சரியான ஒரு மார்க்கத்தை கண்டுகொண்டு, மனம் அந்த தன்னுணர்வு “நான்”ஐ நழுவவிடாமல் முழுமையாக பற்றுகிறது. உண்மையான “நான்”ஐ பற்றிய கணத்தில், கடலை

தொட்ட நதி நீர் அந்த கடலாகவே ஆகின்றதைப் போல, பற்றிய மனமும் அந்த தன்னுணர்வு "நானாகவே" மாறி வர்ணனைக்கு அப்பாற்பட்ட மௌனத்தையும் சாந்தியையும் அடைகிறது. சாந்தியின் ஆனந்தத்தை சுவைத்ததின் "விளைவாக" புற பொருள்களின் மீதான பற்று மனதிலிருந்து தாமாக விலகுகிறது. இதுவே துறவறம்." என ஞானியானவர் எடுத்துரைத்தார். முகத்திலே ஆனந்த கண்ணீர் வழிய, கைகூப்பி, தமக்கு மெய்ஞானத்தை போதிக்கும் படி ஞானியிடம் வேண்டினார் அரசர்.

ஞானி - இவ்வுலகம் யாது? வாழ்வு என்பது என்ன? பிறப்புக்கு முன்னாள் நான் எங்கிருந்தேன்? நான் எவ்வாறு திடீரென இந்த அகிலத்தில் தோன்றினேன்? உறங்கும்போது நான் எங்கு மறைந்தேன்? "நான்" என்பது யாது? எந்த இடத்தில் இந்த "நான்" என்பது இவ்வுடலில் இருக்கிறது? இறைவன் என ஒருவர் உண்மையில் இருக்கிறாரா? போன்ற கேள்விகள் ஒருவருக்கு உண்மையாக எழும்பொழுது, அதற்கான தீர்வை ஒருவர் உண்மையாகவே தேட முற்படுகிறார். அத்தகைய உண்மைத் தன்மையோடு விளங்கும் ஒருவர்க்கு இறைவன் சரியான

நேரத்தில், சரியான வகையில் தோன்றி, மெய்யான ஞானத்தை சற்றே சுவைக்கச் செய்து, அந்த ஞானம் நித்தியமாக நிலைபெற, அந்த குறிப்பிட்ட நபர் பின்பற்ற வேண்டிய உரிய பாதையை காண்பித்து அருள் புரிகிறார். அதன் பிற்பாடு, அந்த மனிதர், பின்பற்றப்பட வேண்டிய அப்பாதையில் தனது பயணத்தை ஒவ்வொரு அங்குலமும் இறைவனின் துணையோடே பயணிக்கலாகிறார்.

அரசர் - அனைத்து மறை நூல்களும், வீடுபேறு அடைய, எண்ணங்களின் அழிவை உறுதி செய்கிறது. அவ்வாறெனில், அது நல்ல எண்ணங்களின் அழிவையும் குறிக்கிறதா?

ஞானி - ஒரு வியாபாரி, தொலைவில் இருக்கும் ஒரு நகரத்தில் தனது வியாபாரத்தை முடித்துக்கொண்டு நிறைய செல்வங்களுடன் தனது சொந்த ஊருக்கு திரும்பிக் கொண்டிருந்தார். ஓரிடத்தில் திடீரென மூன்று திருடர்கள் சற்றும் எதிர்பார்க்காத நிலையில் அந்த வியாபாரியை ஒரு அடர்ந்த காட்டிற்குள் கடத்திச் சென்றுவிட்டனர். காட்டின்

நடுவே அந்த மூன்று திருடர்களும் அவரிடத்தில் இருந்த அனைத்து செல்வங்களையும் முழுவதுமாக பறித்துக் கொண்டனர். பறித்த பிறகு, முதல் திருடன், தான் மறைத்து வைத்திருந்த கத்தியை எடுத்து வியாபாரியை கொல்ல முற்பட்டான். மற்ற இரு திருடர்களும் அவனை தடுத்து நிறுத்தி, நாம் அனைத்து செல்வங்களையும் பறித்து விட்டோம். இப்போது இவரை கொல்வது என்பது தேவையற்ற ஒன்று என முதல் திருடனை சமாதானம் செய்தனர். ஆனால் முதல் திருடன், இவர்களின் கூற்றை மறுத்து, இவரை உயிருடன் நாம் விட்டுவிட்டால், பிறகு இவர் ஊர் மக்களிடம் நம்மை காட்டிக் கொடுத்து விடுவார் என பதிலுரைத்தான். இதற்கு இரண்டாம் திருடன், அப்படியென்றால் இவரை ஒரு மரத்தில் கட்டிப்போட்டுவிட்டு நாம் சென்று விடலாம் என கூறினான். இதுவே சரியான வழி என மூவரும் முடிவெடுத்து, அந்த வியாபாரியை ஒரு மரத்தில் கயிற்றால் இருக கட்டிப் போட்டுவிட்டு அவ்விடம் விட்டு சென்றனர். இருள் சூழ்ந்த அடர்ந்த காட்டிற்கு நடுவே

கட்டிப் போடப்பட்டிருந்த அந்த வியாபாரி, தன்னை விடுவித்துக் கொள்ள மேற்கொண்ட முயற்சிகள் எதுவும் பயனளிக்கவில்லை. செய்வதறியாது திணறினார். துயரத்தின் உச்சியில் தன்னை யாராவது காப்பாற்றும் படி தொடர்ந்து கூச்சலிட்டார். வெகுநேரம் ஆகியும் யாரும் உதவிக்கு வராததால் நம்பிக்கையை இழந்து கதரி அழலானார். திடீரென வியக்கத்தக்க வகையில் அந்த மூன்றாம் திருடன் இவரை நோக்கி நடந்து வந்தார். வந்தவர், வியாபாரியின் கட்டை அவிழ்த்து விட்டு பத்திரமாக வீட்டிற்கு செல்லுங்கள் என கனிவுடன் உரைத்தார். ஆச்சரியத்தில் வியந்த அந்த வியாபாரி தனது மனமார்ந்த நன்றியினை தெரிவித்ததுடன், இந்த இருள் சூழ்ந்த அடர்ந்த காட்டிலிருந்து தனது வீட்டிற்கு செல்ல வழி தெரியவில்லை எனவும், தனக்கு தயை கூர்ந்து வழி காட்ட வேண்டும் எனவும் அந்த திருடனிடத்தில் பணிவாக கேட்டுக் கொண்டார். அந்த திருடன், வழியை காண்பிக்கிறேன் என ஒப்புக்கொண்டு இந்த வியாபாரியின் கையை பிடித்துக் கொண்டு வழிநடத்திச்

செல்லலானார். நீண்ட பயணத்திற்கு பின்பு அடர்ந்த காட்டிலிருந்து அந்த வியாபாரியை வெளியே அழைத்து வந்து, அவரது வீட்டிற்கு செல்லும் பிரதான சாலையை காண்பித்து, இங்கிருந்து நீங்கள் வீட்டிற்கு செல்லுங்கள் என கூறினான். வியாபாரி, கண்ணீர் மல்க நன்றி உணர்வுடன் அந்த திருடனை கட்டி அனைத்து, தனது வீட்டிற்கு விருந்தினராக வரவேண்டும் என அன்புடன் வேண்டி விரும்பி கேட்டுக் கொண்டார். அந்த திருடன் இவரது இரு கைகளையும் பற்றிக்கொண்டு, "ஐயா, உங்கள் அன்பான அழைப்பை என்னால் புரிந்துகொள்ள முடிகிறது. இருப்பினும், விருந்தாளியாக தங்கள் வீட்டிற்கு வர எனக்கு அருகதை கிடையாது. அது மட்டுமல்ல, உங்கள் ஊருக்குள் மக்களின் முன்னிலையில் வரவும் எனக்கு அதிகாரம் இல்லை. ஏனெனில், நானும் ஒரு திருடனே!" என்றார்.

இங்கே, இந்த வியாபாரிதான் ஜீவன். அந்த மூன்று திருடர்கள் சத்துவ, ரஜோ மற்றும் தமஸ் ஆகிய மனதின் மூன்று குணாதிசயங்கள் ஆகும்.

அடர்ந்த காடு என்பது மாயை அல்லது அறியாமை ஆகும். வியாபாரி வைத்திருந்த செல்வங்கள் என்பது ஜீவன் சுமந்து கொண்டு இருக்கும் கர்ம வினைகள். பேராசை, பொறாமை, தீய எண்ணம் போன்ற அழிவை உண்டு செய்யும் தமஸ் குணம் ஜீவனை கொல்ல முயற்சித்தது. அறிவு மற்றும் ஆற்றல் இருந்த போதிலும், அதிகாரம், ஆசை, குழப்பம் போன்றவற்றில் சுழன்று கொண்டிருக்கும் ரஜோ குணம் ஜீவனை சிறையில் வைத்தது. ஆக்கபூர்வமானதும்,கருணைவாய்ந்ததும்,தெளிந்த சிந்தனை மற்றும் உள்ளுணர்வை பெற்றிருக்கும் சத்துவ குணம், ஜீவனுக்கு வீடுபேற்றை அடையும் முக்திக்கான வழியினை காண்பித்த போதிலும், அந்த சத்துவ குணத்திற்கும் கூட மெய்ஞானத்தில் இடமில்லை. காரணம், அதுவும் கூட அறியாமை என்னும் வனத்தைச் சார்ந்ததே.

அரசர் - வீடுபேறு பெற்று முக்தி அடைய, ஒருவர் இழைத்த அனைத்து முற்கால செயல்களின் விளைவுகளை அவருக்கே அனுபவங்களாக வழங்கி அவரின் கர்ம வினைகள் யாவும் பறிக்கப்படுமெனில், முடிவற்ற அலைகளாய் நொடிப்பொழுதும் எழும்பி விழும் “செயல்களில்” இருந்து ஒருவர் எவ்வாறு விடுபடுவது?

ஞானி - "செயல் புரிபவர் நான் இல்லை, சாட்சாத் அந்த இறைவனே" என்பதை தெள்ளத் தெளிவாக உணரும்போது "நானே என் செயலுக்கு கர்த்தா" என்ற அறியாமை முடிவுக்கு வருகிறது. இதன் விளைவாக ஒருவரின் கர்ம வினைகள் யாவும் முடிவுறுகிறது.

அரசர் - இறைவன் தான் உண்மையில் செயல் புரிபவர் என்ற போதிலும், நாம் தான் செயல் புரிகிறோம் என்ற உணர்வு ஏன் நம்முள் எழுகிறது?

ஞானி - நம்முள் இருந்து எழும் எண்ணங்களையும் செயல்களையும் நிதானமாகவும் துல்லியமாகவும் நாம் தொடர்ந்து கவனிக்காததின் விளைவாக எழுந்த அறியாமையே இதற்கு காரணம்.

அரசர் - இந்த அறியாமையில் இருந்து விடுபடுவது எவ்வாறு?

ஞானி - இறைவனை 'பற்றி' அவரோடு ஒன்றி இருப்பதே, அறியாமையில் இருந்து விடுபடும் மார்க்கம் ஆகும்.

அரசர் - இறைவனை எவ்வாறு 'பற்றி' அவரோடு ஒன்றி இருப்பது?

ஞானி - உடலின் அனைத்து அசைவுகளையும் இறைவனே செய்கிறார் என்பதனால், அடுத்த நொடி உங்கள் உடலை, அகத்தில் இருக்கும் இறைவன் எவ்வாறு அசைக்கவிருக்கிறார் என்பதனை வெறுமனே பார்த்துக் கொண்டு இருப்பது, இறைவனோடு ஒன்றி இருப்பது மற்றும் இறைவனை பற்றுதல் ஆகும்.

அரசர் - இவ்வாறு ஒன்றி இருக்கும் பொழுது ஒரு ஜீவனுக்கு என்ன நேர்கிறது?

ஞானி - உரிய நேரத்தில் மெய்ஞான கதவு திறக்கப்படுகிறது.

அரசர் - அந்த கதவு திறக்கும்போது ஒரு ஜீவன் எதை பெறுகிறது?

ஞானி - மகா உன்னதமான சத்தியத்தின் தரிசனத்தை பெறுகிறது.

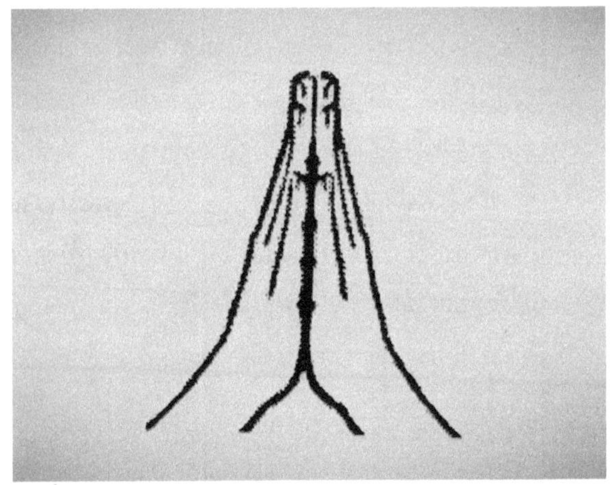

www.ingramcontent.com/pod-product-compliance
Lightning Source LLC
LaVergne TN
LVHW091046150826
845673LV00002B/476

* 9 7 9 8 8 9 2 3 3 4 7 8 5 *